The Automatic Wealth System

Building Money Habits That Don't Rely on Willpower

Daniel Cross

First edition, 2026

Published by Daniel Cross

Contents

Foreword

I spent three years building spreadsheets for people who didn't need spreadsheets. They needed fewer decisions.

Every client who sat across from me knew, in general terms, what they were supposed to do with their money. Save more. Invest consistently. Stop leaking cash to subscriptions nobody used. None of that was news to them. What they lacked wasn't information — it was a system that didn't require them to remember, decide, and act, correctly, every single month, for thirty years straight.

That's an impossible standard. Nobody clears it. The people I watched actually build wealth weren't more disciplined than everyone else — they'd just engineered discipline out of the equation. Money moved before they could talk themselves out of it. The good decision was the default, not a choice they had to keep making.

This book is the mechanics of that engineering. Not motivation, not mindset — plumbing. Where the money goes, in what order, on what trigger, and how you build a structure that keeps working on the weeks you're too busy, too tired, or too distracted to think about it at all.

I still remember the specific afternoon this became obvious to me. Two clients, same week, nearly identical incomes. One had a color-coded spreadsheet and a genuine intention to save more. The other had never opened a budgeting app in her life, but her paycheck split itself into four accounts the moment it landed, and had for six years. She wasn't more careful with money. She'd simply never had to be, because the carefulness had already been built into the structure before her first coffee of the morning. That gap — between a system that depends on you and a system that doesn't — is the entire subject of what follows.

I'm not going to tell you why you procrastinate on your finances. Other books do that well, and the psychology is real. This one starts after that conversation is over — once you've decided you want the system, here's exactly how to build it, account by account, transfer by transfer, so willpower never has to show up again.

— Daniel Cross

Introduction

Here's the uncomfortable truth about most financial advice: it assumes you're going to keep making the right decision, over and over, for the rest of your life. Track every expense. Resist every impulse purchase. Remember to move money into savings before you spend it. Rebalance your investments on schedule. Cancel the subscriptions you forgot you had. Do this every month, forever, without fail.

Nobody does this. Not because people are lazy or lack character — because it's a bad design. You wouldn't build a bridge that only stays up if every driver remembers to steer carefully. You'd build guardrails. That's what this book is: guardrails for your money, engineered so the correct financial behavior happens automatically, and the incorrect one takes active effort to reach.

This isn't a book about budgeting harder. It's not about finding more willpower, tracking every latte, or feeling guilty when you slip. It's a book about designing a system — a specific arrangement of accounts, transfers, timing, and triggers

— so that saving, investing, and spending wisely become the path of least resistance instead of a daily fight against your own impulses.

The core idea is simple and it's not new: pay yourself first. Move money toward your future before you have the chance to spend it on your present. What this book adds is the part almost nobody explains well — the actual mechanics of how to do that so it survives contact with real life. Real paychecks that don't arrive on the same day every month. Real income that varies if you freelance or run a business. Real emergencies that blow through your buffer. Real raises that quietly get absorbed into a slightly nicer lifestyle instead of a slightly bigger savings rate.

You'll notice this book doesn't spend much time asking why you avoid your finances, why a full inbox of statements makes you anxious, or why the same conversation about money keeps getting postponed. That's real, and it's worth understanding — but it's not what this book does. This book assumes you already know, in the abstract, what you're supposed to do. The problem isn't the knowing. It's that knowing has never been the thing standing between you and a functioning system. A system doesn't ask you to remember your intentions every month. It just runs.

Here's what's ahead. The first few chapters build the foundation: the real math behind pay-yourself-first, and the account architecture that makes automatic allocation possible in the first place. From there, the book covers automating your investment contributions, auditing and killing recurring costs without a monthly fight, and — critically — how to run this entire system if your income doesn't arrive in tidy, predictable paychecks. Later chapters cover raising your savings rate automatically as your income grows, building in enough flexibility that the system doesn't snap under real-life pressure, the tactical mistakes that quietly break automated systems, and what to do when the system fails outright — a layoff, a medical bill, an emergency that blows past every buffer you built.

A word on how to read this book. Each chapter follows the same shape: it names a situation you'll recognize, explains the actual mechanics of why the standard approach fails there, hands you a concrete framework or script you can put in place this week, and then walks through a worked example with real numbers, so the framework isn't left abstract. You don't need to implement all ten chapters simultaneously to get value from this book. The account architecture in Chapter 3 is the load-bearing piece almost everything else attaches to, so it's worth building first regardless of where your specific situation sits — variable income, a fresh start, or an existing system you're trying to fix. From there, work through whichever chapters match your actual situation first, and treat the rest as reference material to return to as your circumstances change.

A word on what this book won't do. It won't tell you exactly what percentage to save, because that number depends on your fixed costs, your income stability, and your goals in a way no book can responsibly generalize. It won't recommend specific banks, apps, or investment products, because those change constantly and a recommendation that's current today reads as stale advice within a couple of years. What it will do is teach you the mechanics well enough that you can make those specific choices yourself, correctly, regardless of which bank, which app, or which year you're reading this in. The mechanics — sequencing, separation, automatic triggers, tested percentages

— don't expire. That's deliberate, and it's the entire reason this book is organized around mechanics rather than a checklist of today's best financial products.

A final word on who this book is for. It's for the person with a stable salaried job trying to finally get saving to actually happen, consistently, instead of in occasional bursts of resolve. It's equally for the freelancer or business owner whose income swings enough that "just save 15%" has never made practical sense as advice, and who needs a structure built specifically for that reality rather than borrowed uncritically from a salaried template. It's for the person starting from zero, with no existing system to speak of, and just as much for the person with an existing system that's quietly stopped working and needs a specific, chapter-by-chapter diagnosis of where it broke. If any of those describes you, the mechanics ahead are built to work for your specific situation, not a generic average of everyone's.

By the end, you won't have a new list of things to remember to do. You'll have a system that does them without you.

Let's build it.

Chapter 1 — The Myth of Discipline

Why "Just Be Better With Money" Was Never a Real Plan

Picture the standard advice: make a budget, track every dollar, resist temptation, save what's left over. It sounds reasonable. It's also a plan that depends on you performing perfectly, every day, for decades, with no bad weeks. That's not a financial strategy. That's a hope.

Willpower is a terrible foundation for a financial system because willpower is not a stable resource. It's highest when you're rested, well-fed, and not stressed — and lowest exactly when money matters most: after a hard week, during a health scare, in the run-up to a holiday, in the middle of a life transition. The moments you most need to make a good financial decision are statistically the moments you're least equipped to make one. Building a savings plan that depends on willpower means building a plan that's engineered to fail during exactly the periods it needs to hold.

Consider what a willpower-dependent savings plan is actually asking of you across a full working life. Not one good decision, but the same correct decision, repeated without fail, across roughly four hundred to six hundred separate paychecks over a thirty- to forty-year career — each one arriving during a different week, a different mood, a different set of competing pressures, some of them genuinely difficult weeks with real emergencies attached. A plan that requires all four hundred to six hundred of those decisions to land correctly isn't a modest ask dressed up as achievable. It's asking for a flawless streak longer than almost anyone actually sustains for anything in life, financial or otherwise. Framed this way, the standard advice's real failure rate stops looking like a personal shortcoming shared by an unusually undisciplined subset of people, and starts looking like exactly what you'd expect from asking an entire population to clear an unreasonably long streak of individually fragile decisions.

Compare that to the "save what's left over" model most people default to. At the end of the month, whatever's still in checking either gets saved or it doesn't. The problem isn't that people are bad at this — it's that "what's left over" is, structurally, whatever spending expanded to fill. Income rises, spending quietly rises to match it, and the leftover — the thing that was supposed to become savings — stays close to zero no matter how much you earn. This isn't a character flaw. It's what happens when the "savings" step comes last in the sequence instead of first.

What's actually happening

Every dollar that touches your main checking account before it's allocated is a dollar that has to survive a decision. Should this go to savings, or can it wait? Should I transfer this now, or is it fine to do it Friday? Each of those micro-decisions is small, but they compound — dozens of times a month, for years — and each one is an opportunity for the money to just... stay where it is. Convenience always wins ties. If saving requires an active step and spending requires none, spending wins by default, not by choice.

This is the actual mechanism behind "I make good money but somehow never save any of it." It's not usually overspending on anything specific. It's that the money sat in an account with no job assigned to it, and undirected money gets absorbed into whatever's convenient — a slightly better dinner, a slightly less delayed purchase, a slightly higher tier subscription. None of these decisions feel irresponsible in the moment. They just quietly consume the gap between income and savings, one convenience at a time.

The fix isn't more self-control at the moment of temptation. It's removing the moment of temptation from the sequence entirely. If the money is already gone — already moved to a savings or investment account before you ever see it sitting in checking — there's no decision left to make. You can't spend money you never had access to in the first place. That's the entire logic this book is built on: don't try to out-discipline the decision point. Delete the decision point.

It's worth pausing on why this particular failure is so easy to misdiagnose as a personal shortcoming rather than a structural one. When savings don't accumulate the way someone intended, the natural conclusion is usually "I need to be more careful" or "I need more willpower" — an internal, character-based explanation. But the actual mechanism described above has nothing to do with character. It's a predictable, structural outcome of a specific sequencing choice, and it produces the same result in nearly anyone subjected to it, regardless of how disciplined they consider themselves in other areas of life. Recognizing this distinction matters because it changes where you look for the fix. A character-based diagnosis sends you looking for more resolve, more tracking, more vigilance — solutions aimed at the wrong layer of the problem, per the argument made throughout this chapter. A structural diagnosis sends you looking for a different sequence, a different set of defaults, a different account architecture — solutions aimed at the actual cause. This book is built entirely around the second diagnosis.

The framework: automate the decision, not the behavior

Most advice tries to change your behavior at the point of temptation — spend less, want less, resist more. This book takes a different approach: change the *structure* so the temptation never gets the chance to operate on your money at all. There are three components to this, and they show up in every chapter that follows:

1. Move money before you see it. Any transfer that depends on you remembering to do it, after the money has already landed in your spending account, is competing with every other claim on that money. Transfers that happen automatically, on payday, before the balance is even visible to you as "spendable," never have to compete with anything.

2. Separate accounts by job, not by amount. A single checking account holding rent money, grocery money, savings, and fun money side by side is a single account with four jobs and no way to tell them apart. When every dollar in an account looks the same, your brain treats it the same — which means savings money looks exactly as spendable as grocery money right up until it's gone. Separate accounts create a visual and structural boundary that a single balance never can.

3. Make the automatic path the correct path. The system should be built so that doing nothing — literally taking no action at all in a given month — still results in the right outcome: money saved, bills paid, investments funded. Willpower should only be required to *override* the system in an unusual month, never to *operate* it in a normal one.

Worked example

Consider two people earning the same $5,000 monthly take-home pay. The first keeps everything in one checking account and tries to save "whatever's left" after bills and spending. Some months that's $400. Some months it's $50. Some months a bigger-than-expected week eats into next month's rent, and there's a scramble to cover it. Across a year, the total saved is unpredictable and generally low, because savings only happens with whatever attention and willpower survive the month.

The second person sets up an automatic transfer of $750 — 15% of take-home pay — to a separate savings account on the same day their paycheck lands, before any bills are paid and before the money is visible as spendable in their main account. Their remaining $4,250 covers the exact same bills and the exact same lifestyle the first person has. The difference isn't income. It's not even spending discipline in the moment-to-moment sense. It's that the second person's savings happened *before* the month had a chance to compete for that money, and the first person's savings had to survive the entire month intact before it counted.

Over a year, the second person saves a predictable $9,000. The first person's total depends entirely on how the year went — and in most years, "how the year went" quietly erodes toward zero. That gap isn't a gap in character. It's a gap in sequencing. The rest of this book is about building that sequencing correctly, account by account, so it runs the same way whether you're having a great month or a terrible one.

Why "motivation" articles keep missing the actual lever

Search for financial advice and you'll find no shortage of content urging you to build better money habits through sheer resolve — track every purchase, set intentions, visualize your goals. None of it is dishonest exactly, but it's aimed at the wrong layer of the problem. Willpower operates at the level of individual decisions. A system operates at the level of the environment those decisions get made in. You can spend years trying to win the individual decisions — and some months you will — but you're playing a game you're guaranteed to lose eventually, because the game runs forever and willpower doesn't hold steady forever. Change the environment instead, and you don't need to win every individual decision anymore. The environment does the winning for you, automatically, on the months you'd otherwise have lost.

This is also why motivation-driven attempts tend to produce a recognizable pattern: a burst of enthusiasm, a few weeks of manually tracking everything and hitting every savings target, followed by a quiet return to whatever the old pattern was, usually within two or three months. That's not a personal failure. It's what happens to any strategy built entirely on a renewable-but-finite resource, applied against an environment that hasn't changed at all. The spending paths are still frictionless and the savings paths are still absent. Motivation faded; the underlying structure that made saving hard and spending easy never did.

A second worked example: two incomes, one household

The mechanic scales the same way across a household with more than one income. Consider two people sharing expenses, earning $4,200 and $3,400 a month respectively after tax, for a combined $7,600. Rather than merging into one undifferentiated pool and hoping "we'll save what's left," they set two parallel automatic transfers, each sized to its own income: 12% from the first ($504) and 12% from the second ($408), both firing the day each paycheck lands, both routing into the shared account structure Chapter 3 builds.

Keeping the percentages tied to each person's own income, rather than negotiating one combined number after both paychecks land, matters for the same reason as everything else in this chapter: each transfer competes with nothing, because it happens before either paycheck is fully visible as a joint, spendable pool. If the household instead waited until both incomes landed and then tried to jointly decide how much to move to savings, that decision would have to survive two people's differing spending instincts and a conversation that has to happen fresh every month — reintroducing the exact decision-point vulnerability this chapter exists to eliminate. Automate each stream at the source, before it merges into a shared balance, and there's no monthly negotiation left to have.

The friction test: a diagnostic you can run on any financial habit

Everything in this book comes back to one underlying question, and it's worth naming explicitly so you can apply it to situations this book doesn't cover directly: for any given financial behavior, which side of it has more friction — doing the right thing, or doing the convenient thing? If spending is one tap on a saved card and saving requires opening a second app, logging in, and manually initiating a transfer, the friction is stacked against you before you've made a single decision, no matter how motivated you feel that particular week. If saving is automatic and unspending — pulling money back out of a buffer or investment account — requires a deliberate, multi-step transfer, the friction is stacked in your favor instead.

Run this test on any recurring financial behavior you're trying to change, not just the ones this book covers directly.

Trying to eat out less? The friction test asks whether ordering food is easier or harder than the alternative you're aiming for. Trying to stop impulse-buying online? It asks whether checkout is one click or requires re-entering payment details every time. The mechanism is identical to everything in this chapter — you're not trying to become a person with more resistance to temptation, you're trying to rearrange the environment so resistance is needed less often, on both sides of the ledger, spending and saving alike.

What a full paycheck cycle looks like once this is running

It's worth picturing the actual sequence of events once the system in this book is fully in place, because it looks almost boring — which is the intended outcome, not a shortcoming. Payday arrives. Before you've opened your banking app, before you've made a single decision, a series of transfers has already executed: pay-yourself-first money has moved to buffer, goal, and investment accounts; a fixed amount has moved to the spending account tied to your everyday card; fixed costs are already scheduled on autopay from the bills account. By the time you actually check your balance, hours or days later, everything that needed to happen already has. The only thing left for you to do is spend, within the honest number the spending account shows you, and to conduct periodic reviews — quarterly, per Chapter 9 — rather than daily vigilance. That shift, from constant low-grade financial attention to occasional scheduled review, is the actual product this book is building toward. Not more money by itself — a life that requires dramatically less ongoing decision-making to produce the same disciplined outcome.

Why this chapter comes first

Every subsequent chapter in this book is, in one sense, a variation on the argument made here: pay-yourself-first mechanics (Chapter 2), account separation (Chapter 3), investment automation (Chapter 4), the subscription audit (Chapter 5), variable-income handling (Chapter 6), escalation (Chapter 7), flexibility (Chapter 8), and even the failure protocol (Chapter 10) are all applications of the same underlying move — identify a decision point that currently depends on willpower, and rebuild the environment around it so the decision no longer has to be made, or is made once instead of monthly. If this chapter's core claim doesn't land, the rest of the book will read as a list of disconnected tactics rather than a coherent system. If it does land, everything that follows will feel like the obvious, almost inevitable consequence of taking the claim seriously — which is exactly how a well-designed system should feel once it's built: less like a clever trick and more like the only sensible way the pieces could have fit together.

One last framing worth carrying forward: none of this requires you to distrust your own judgment in general. It requires you to recognize one specific, well-documented limitation — that judgment exercised repeatedly, under varying conditions, over long stretches of time, degrades in predictable ways — and to build around that one limitation rather than around your character as a whole. You can be a fundamentally disciplined, capable person and still benefit enormously from removing decisions you don't need to be making manually. The two aren't in tension. A pilot who trusts an autopilot system for a six-hour flight isn't confessing incompetence — they're recognizing that sustained manual vigilance over a long, repetitive stretch is a worse tool for the job than a system built to handle it. This book asks you to extend that same recognition to your finances.

The gap between knowing and doing, made concrete

Ask most people whether they should be saving a consistent percentage of every paycheck, and almost everyone agrees, immediately, without hesitation. Ask the same people whether they actually do it, consistently, every single month, and the honest answer is far more mixed. That gap — between what people know and what people actually do, month after month — is the entire subject of this book, and it's worth being precise about what closes it and what doesn't. More financial education doesn't close it; the people struggling to save consistently mostly already know they should be saving. More motivation doesn't close it either, or doesn't close it durably, for the reasons covered earlier in this chapter. What closes it is removing the gap's actual mechanism: the fact that knowing what to do and doing it are two entirely separate events, separated by a decision point, and that decision point can simply be deleted.

This is why the account architecture and automatic transfers in this book aren't a workaround or a compromise — they're the direct, structural answer to the actual problem. Not "how do I become someone who reliably does the thing I know I should do," which is a much harder and slower question with an uncertain answer, but "how do I build a system where the thing that should happen, happens, regardless of whether I'm in the mood to make it happen that particular week." The second question has a concrete, buildable answer. That's what the rest of this book delivers, chapter by chapter, mechanic by mechanic.

What "automatic" actually means, precisely

It's worth being exact about the word this book leans on constantly, because "automatic" gets used loosely elsewhere in ways that don't hold up. An automatic transfer isn't automatic if it requires you to log in and manually approve it each time, even if the approval takes ten seconds — that ten-second decision point is still a decision point, still subject to a bad week, still capable of being skipped. It isn't automatic if it depends on a notification you have to act on, since a missed or ignored notification produces the same outcome as no automation at all. True automation, in the sense this book uses the word throughout, means the transfer executes on its own, on a schedule, without requiring any action, approval, or even attention from you at the moment it happens. You should be able to ignore your finances entirely for a month and have the correct things still occur. That's the bar. Anything short of it is a partial improvement, worth having, but not the full mechanism this book is describing — and worth eventually upgrading to the fully automatic version wherever your bank or platform's features allow it.

Reading this book if you've already tried and failed at automation before

If you've set up automatic transfers in the past and had the system quietly fall apart — a transfer that got paused during a tight month and never restarted, a percentage that made sense at one income and became unworkable at another, a buffer account that slowly got spent down to nothing — this book isn't asking you to try the same thing again with more resolve. Every one of those failure modes has a specific chapter addressing exactly why it happened and how to build around it structurally: an untested percentage against a bad month is Chapter 2's problem to fix, a buffer that became too easy to spend from is Chapter 3's, a rate that never adjusted to a new life stage is Chapter 7's, a pause that never got reversed is Chapter 8's. A previous attempt at automation that failed isn't evidence that automation doesn't work for you. It's usually evidence that one specific piece of the structure was missing, and the rest of this book exists to identify precisely which piece that was.

The cost of doing nothing while you wait for the "right" moment to start

There's a specific, quiet cost to delaying the start of this system that's worth naming directly, because the delay itself rarely feels like a decision — it feels like waiting for more clarity, a better income, a calmer season of life, before starting something this comprehensive. But every month spent waiting for ideal conditions is a month where the old pattern — undirected spending, savings as a residual, investment contributions left to chance — continues running by default, simply because no new structure has replaced it yet. There's no neutral holding pattern while you wait for a better time to build this system; the old, unstructured pattern is still actively running the whole time you're waiting, producing its usual outcome. The version of this system you can build today, imperfectly, with the numbers you actually have right now, and refine at your first quarterly review, will always outperform the theoretically superior version you're waiting to have the "right" circumstances to build. Chapter 4's late-start worked example makes this same point about investing specifically; it's worth taking as a general operating principle for the whole book, not just that one chapter.

Small systems beat large intentions

There's a related instinct worth naming and setting aside before moving into the rest of this book: the pull toward designing the complete, final, perfect version of this system before implementing any of it — every account opened, every percentage finalized, every contingency planned, before a single transfer actually goes live. This instinct feels responsible, but it functions as another form of the same delay covered above, dressed up as thoroughness rather than hesitation. A single automatic transfer, imperfectly sized, moving real money on a real schedule starting this week, teaches you more about what your actual system needs than an unlimited amount of planning ever will, because it generates real feedback — an actual month's worth of data about whether the number holds — that no amount of forecasting on paper can substitute for. Start with the smallest version of this system you can put in place this week: one account, one transfer, one tested percentage. Build the rest around what that first piece teaches you, rather than trying to design the complete architecture from a standing start with no real data yet to build it against.

Chapter 2 — The Pay-Yourself-First Mechanics

Why the Order of Operations Matters More Than the Amount

"Pay yourself first" is a phrase you've probably heard a hundred times, usually without much explanation of what it actually means mechanically. Here it is in plain terms: before you pay a single bill, before you buy groceries, before anything else touches your paycheck, a fixed portion of it moves into savings or investments. Everything else — rent, food, all discretionary spending — gets built around whatever's left, not the other way around.

This sounds like a small reordering, but it changes the entire psychology and math of saving. When saving comes last, it's treated as optional — the thing that happens if there's room for it. When saving comes first, it's treated as a fixed cost, exactly like rent. You don't "decide" whether to pay rent each month depending on how you feel; it's simply gone before you can consider not paying it. Pay-yourself-first applies that same non-negotiable status to your future, not just your landlord.

What's actually happening

Behavioral economics doesn't need a citation for this one — you can verify it against your own bank statement. Money that's visible in your checking account gets mentally categorized as "available," regardless of what it's actually meant for. If your paycheck lands and your savings goal hasn't been extracted yet, that entire paycheck reads as spendable, even the part you intended to save. Every purchase decision you make for the rest of the month is drawing against a number that's artificially inflated by money that was never really yours to spend.

Flip the order, and the math flips with it. If 15% moves out automatically before you see anything, your checking account balance is now an *accurate* number — it reflects exactly what's actually available for spending. You're not fighting the temptation to spend savings money, because savings money is no longer sitting in the account where spending happens. This is the single biggest reason pay-yourself-first outperforms budget-then-save: it doesn't rely on you correctly identifying, in the moment, which dollars are "allowed" to be spent. It makes that identification happen once, automatically, before spending decisions even start.

This also explains why traditional budgeting, done conscientiously, still so often fails to produce consistent savings even when someone genuinely tracks every category diligently. A detailed budget can tell you, after the fact, exactly where last month's money went — but it does nothing, on its own, to change the order in which that money became available in the first place. Tracking spending more precisely doesn't alter the sequence; it just produces a more accurate record of a sequence that was already working against you. Pay-yourself-first isn't a more detailed way of tracking the same process. It's a different process, one where the number you're tracking against — your checking account balance — was never inflated by savings money in the first place, because that money left before tracking even needed to begin.

The framework: setting your real percentage

The common advice is "save 20% of your income," and it's a reasonable starting anchor, but treating it as a universal rule misses the actual mechanics. What matters is setting a percentage you can sustain through a bad month without breaking the system — because a savings rate that gets suspended every time cash gets tight isn't really automatic at all; it's just optional saving with extra steps.

Work the number backward instead of forward:

1. **Start from your true fixed costs.** Rent or mortgage, utilities, insurance, minimum debt payments, groceries at a realistic (not bare-bones) level. This is the floor your automated system must never touch. 2. **Test a percentage against your worst realistic month, not your average month.** If your income varies at all, or if you've had months with unplanned expenses, don't set your pay-yourself-first rate against a clean, best-case paycheck. Set it against the month rent was late, the car needed a repair, or income dipped. If the percentage still holds without needing an emergency override, it's sustainable. If it doesn't, it's too high to automate reliably — you'll end up manually pausing it, which defeats the entire point. 3. **Start below what feels aggressive, and raise it later.** A 10% automatic rate you never touch beats a 25% rate you disable three months in. Chapter 7 covers exactly how to raise this rate

over time without ever having to consciously decide to do it — but the starting number should be one you can leave alone. 4. **Split the percentage across purposes before it lands anywhere.** Not all of your pay-yourself-first money is doing the same job. Some of it is short-term insurance (an emergency buffer), some of it is medium-term goals, and some of it is long-term investing. Chapter 3 builds the account structure for this split; for now, know that "15% to savings" usually isn't one transfer — it's several, each with a different destination and purpose.

Worked example

Take someone earning $4,800 a month after tax, with $3,400 in genuinely fixed costs including a realistic grocery and transportation budget. That leaves $1,400 of flexible room. Rather than trying to save "whatever's left" from that $1,400 — which, per Chapter 1, tends to erode toward a much smaller number — they set an automatic pay-yourself-first rate of 12% of take-home pay: $576 a month, moved out on payday before anything else happens.

That $576 splits three ways automatically: $150 to a buffer account until it hits a three-month reserve, $150 to a medium-term goal account, and the remaining $276 to an investment account. Of the original $4,800, $3,400 covers fixed costs and $576 moves out as pay-yourself-first, leaving $824 for genuinely discretionary spending — dining out, entertainment, upgrades, the stuff that makes a budget livable rather than punishing.

Over a year, this produces a guaranteed $6,912 moved into savings and investments — not a hoped-for number, not a number that depends on twelve consecutive months of discipline, but a number that happens whether or not this was a good year. That's the entire value of the mechanic: it converts an aspiration into an arithmetic certainty.

Handling pay schedules that don't land monthly

Not everyone gets paid once a month on a clean, predictable date. Biweekly pay produces twenty-six paychecks a year instead of twelve — meaning two months out of twelve carry a third paycheck your monthly budget doesn't normally account for. Weekly pay compounds this further. The mechanic doesn't change, but the trigger does: rather than anchoring the pay-yourself-first percentage to "the month," anchor it to "the paycheck." A 12% transfer fires every time income lands, regardless of how many times that happens in a given month. The two "extra" paychecks a biweekly schedule produces each year become two extra automatic pay-yourself-first transfers, rather than two months where the system has to guess whether this paycheck is a normal one or a bonus one. This removes an entire category of manual judgment call — you never have to decide, paycheck by paycheck, whether "this one" counts as extra income to be spent differently. Every paycheck gets treated identically, which is precisely what makes the system automatic rather than semi-automatic.

For anyone paid on inconsistent dates within an otherwise stable job — a date that shifts around weekends or holidays, for instance — the practical fix is to set the automatic transfer a day or two after the *latest* the paycheck could plausibly land, rather than the earliest. A transfer that fires before the money has actually arrived either fails outright or triggers an overdraft, and repeated failures are one of the fastest ways an automated system loses your trust and gets manually disabled. Chapter 6 covers the more extreme version of this problem — genuinely variable income — in full; this is the milder version, where income is reliable but its exact timing isn't, and a small buffer of days in the transfer schedule solves it without needing anything more elaborate.

Addressing the obvious objection: "I need every dollar right now"

This is the most common objection to pay-yourself-first, and it deserves a direct answer rather than a dismissal, because sometimes it's genuinely true. If your fixed costs consume your entire income with nothing left over, no percentage of automatic savings is going to appear out of nowhere — automation redistributes money, it doesn't create it. In that specific situation, the honest starting move isn't to force a savings percentage that will just bounce or overdraft; it's to work the side of the equation this book hasn't covered yet, reducing fixed costs (Chapter 5's audit is a real lever here, even for supposedly non-negotiable recurring costs) or increasing income, before automation has anything to work with.

But it's worth being precise about how rare that situation actually is, versus how often it merely *feels* that way. In most cases where someone says there's nothing left over, what's actually true is that spending has expanded to consume all of it — which is exactly the erosion pattern Chapter 1 described, not a genuine mathematical impossibility. The test is the same one from earlier: look at true fixed costs, the ones that don't move month to month, and compare them honestly to income. If there's a real gap even at a modest percentage — even 5%, even $50 a month — that's not "nothing." A small, sustainable, automatic amount that survives every month beats a larger number that only survives some of them. Start there, and let Chapter 7's escalation mechanic do the work of growing it later, once income rises or fixed costs come down.

How this interacts with existing debt

Pay-yourself-first isn't a replacement for a debt payoff plan, and this book doesn't attempt to relitigate the mechanics of payoff ordering, which is genuinely its own subject. What matters here is sequencing the two correctly rather than treating them as competing claims on the same dollar. A workable default: the pay-yourself-first percentage in this chapter should, at minimum, always capture any employer retirement match available to you (Chapter 4 covers why this is close to a guaranteed return), and beyond that match, money earmarked for debt above a genuinely high interest rate generally take priority over building the percentage in this chapter higher than a modest baseline. Once high-cost debt is cleared, the percentage that had been servicing it becomes a natural, ready-made source for escalating the pay-yourself-first rate — the payment already existed in the budget, its job simply changes from "debt" to "savings," which is a far easier automatic transition than trying to conjure a new percentage from scratch once the debt is gone.

Benchmark percentages, and why none of them are universal

You'll see specific benchmark percentages thrown around in general financial advice — save 10%, save 15%, save 20% — and it's worth understanding why this book resists anchoring hard to any single one of them. These numbers are usually calculated against an average household's average expenses, which may have very little to do with your actual fixed-cost floor, your local cost of living, your income stability, or how many working years you have ahead of you to compound whatever you save. A benchmark percentage is a reasonable starting anchor for comparison, not a target to force onto a budget that can't sustain it. The method in this chapter — testing a specific number against your own worst realistic month — will sometimes land above the common benchmarks and sometimes below them, and either outcome is fine, because the number that matters is the one that survives contact with your actual life, not the one that matches a number you saw in an article.

Percentage versus fixed dollar amount: which to automate

There's a genuine choice buried inside "pay yourself first" that's easy to skip past: should the automated transfer be a fixed percentage of each paycheck, or a fixed dollar amount? Both are valid, and they suit slightly different situations. A percentage scales automatically with income — a raise increases the dollar amount saved without any manual update required, which pairs naturally with the escalation mechanics in Chapter 7, and works well for anyone whose income is likely to grow in the near term. A fixed dollar amount is simpler to plan a budget around, since the discretionary spending amount left over is identical every paycheck rather than shifting slightly with each pay period's exact figure, which can matter for someone whose fixed costs are also fixed dollar amounts and who prefers a completely predictable remainder.

In practice, a percentage is usually the better default specifically because it removes yet another manual step — updating the amount after every raise — from the list of things that require your active attention. A fixed amount isn't wrong, but it reintroduces a small piece of the exact problem this book is trying to eliminate: a number that was correct when it was set and silently becomes less correct as circumstances change, unless someone remembers to revisit it. If you do choose a fixed dollar amount for its predictability, pair it explicitly with the review habit from Chapter 9, since it needs deliberate revisiting in a way a percentage doesn't.

Why "pay yourself first" beats "spend less, then save"

It's worth directly contrasting the sequencing this chapter argues for against the sequencing most budgeting advice implicitly assumes, because the difference is easy to state but easy to underestimate in practice. The conventional approach — track spending across categories, trim where you can, and whatever's left over becomes savings — treats savings as a residual: the output of a subtraction problem that depends on every input being estimated and tracked correctly, every month, for the residual to be accurate. Pay-yourself-first inverts which side of the equation is the residual. Savings becomes an input, fixed and automatic; spending becomes the residual, whatever's left after the more important allocation has already happened.

This inversion matters because residuals are inherently the least protected number in any equation — they absorb every error, every underestimate, every unplanned cost from everywhere else in the calculation. Under the conventional approach, savings absorbs every budgeting mistake made anywhere else in the month. Under pay-yourself-first, spending absorbs those mistakes instead — which is a far less costly place for an error to land, since a slightly tighter discretionary month is a minor inconvenience, while a slightly smaller-than-planned savings contribution, repeated across years, is the actual compounding cost this entire book is trying to prevent. The math in both approaches can, in principle, land at the same number. In practice, over a long enough timeline, they almost never do — because one approach protects the number that matters most from absorbing error, and the other doesn't.

Testing your own number before you automate it

Before setting any pay-yourself-first percentage live, it's worth running a short paper test rather than trusting a number chosen on instinct. Take your worst month from the last twelve to eighteen months — the one with the tightest margin, the unplanned repair, the lightest paycheck, whatever it was — and recalculate it as if the proposed percentage had already been automatically withdrawn before that month's expenses were paid. Would the fixed costs still have cleared? Would there have been a genuine, if uncomfortable, path through the month without touching the buffer? If the answer is yes, even if it was tight, the percentage passes the test and is ready to automate with real confidence. If the answer is no — if that percentage would have caused an overdraft or forced an emergency withdrawal from savings during your actual worst recent month — the number is too aggressive to trust yet, regardless of how reasonable it looks against an average month's numbers. This isn't a discouraging exercise; it's the single fastest way to arrive at a number you'll never need to quietly disable, which is worth far more over a decade than a slightly higher number that gets abandoned after three rocky months.

What "before anything else touches your paycheck" means in practice

The phrase this chapter opened with — before you pay a single bill, before you buy groceries, a fixed portion moves into savings — is a useful mental model, but worth translating into the literal mechanical timing that actually makes it true. In practice, this rarely means the pay-yourself-first transfer executes a fraction of a second before your rent payment; it means both are scheduled to fire on or immediately after payday, in an order set at the bank or platform level so the savings transfer isn't dependent on discretionary spending decisions happening first. Some banks allow explicit transfer-priority ordering; where that's not available, the practical equivalent is simply scheduling the pay-yourself-first transfer for the same day as payday and any bill autopay for a day or two later, so the savings allocation is functionally locked in before bills, groceries, or anything else has the chance to draw down the account first. The exact mechanical implementation will vary by bank, but the underlying goal is constant across all of them: the savings transfer should never be positioned, structurally, as something that happens only if enough is left over after everything else clears.

What happens the first time a transfer bounces

Even a carefully tested percentage will occasionally hit a month where the timing doesn't line up cleanly — a paycheck arrives a day later than usual, a large bill clears earlier than expected, and the pay-yourself-first transfer attempts to fire against a temporarily insufficient balance. This is worth planning for explicitly rather than treating as a sign the whole system has failed. Most banks offer some form of low-balance alert or a brief grace period before an automatic transfer that would overdraw an account is actually rejected; understanding your specific bank's behavior here, in advance, prevents a single timing mismatch from cascading into fees or a moment of panic that undermines confidence in the system. If a transfer does bounce, the correct response is a quick root-cause check — was this a genuine timing fluke, or a sign the percentage itself is miscalibrated against current reality — followed by either a manual one-time correction to that month's timing or, if the bounce reveals a real structural problem, a return to the bad-month test from earlier in this chapter. One bounced transfer is data. It's not, on its own, evidence that automation has failed you.

A short buffer between paycheck and transfer, as standard practice

Where your bank allows it, building in a small, deliberate delay — a day or two — between the moment a paycheck is expected to land and the moment the pay-yourself-first transfer actually fires, absorbs most of the ordinary timing variability covered above before it ever becomes a problem. This isn't in tension with the "before you see it" principle from earlier in the chapter; the money is still moved before it's treated as spendable, and a one- or two-day buffer is far too short a window for the erosion dynamics from Chapter 1 to meaningfully take hold. It simply gives ordinary payroll-processing variability — a holiday shifting a direct deposit by a day, a bank's own processing delay — room to resolve itself before the automated transfer attempts to execute against a balance that hasn't fully landed yet. A small, deliberate buffer here is a minor mechanical convenience, not a compromise of the chapter's core principle.

Chapter 3 — The Account Architecture

Why One Checking Account Can't Do Four Jobs

If you've internalized Chapter 1's core claim — that undifferentiated money gets treated as spendable regardless of its intended purpose — the fix follows directly: money needs to live in accounts that match its job, not just its amount. A single checking account holding rent money, grocery money, an emergency cushion, and a vacation fund side by side isn't a mistake exactly, but it's structurally guaranteed to blur the lines between them. There's no visual, no balance, no signal that separates "spendable" from "already spoken for."

Account architecture is the physical infrastructure that makes automation possible in the first place. Without separate accounts with separate jobs, there's nowhere for pay-yourself-first transfers to land that actually protects the money once it arrives. This chapter is about designing that structure once, so every later automation — investing, bill negotiation, variable income, escalation — has somewhere correct to plug into.

A useful analogy: think of a single undifferentiated checking account as an open-plan office with no walls, where every desk holds a slightly different function — accounting, customer calls, inventory — but nothing physically separates them. Work still technically gets done, but tasks bleed into each other constantly, and it's easy for something urgent-looking at one desk to pull attention away from something quieter but more important at another. The four-account structure this chapter builds is the equivalent of putting up walls: each function gets its own room, with its own door, and crossing from one to another requires an actual, deliberate action rather than just a glance sideways. Nothing about the total amount of money changes when you build this structure. What changes is how easily any given dollar can drift from the job it was meant to do into a job it wasn't.

What's actually happening

The core failure mode of a single-account system isn't overspending in a dramatic sense. It's erosion — money in "savings" getting spent because it was sitting in the same account, with the same visible balance, as everything else, and nothing distinguished it in the moment a purchase decision got made. Mental accounting only works when it's backed by *actual* accounting. You can tell yourself "the last $2,000 in this account is my emergency fund" all you want; if it's sitting in the same account as your grocery money, it will get spent on groceries eventually, because there's no friction between the two.

Separate accounts create that friction. Moving money from a savings account back into checking to cover a purchase is a deliberate, visible action — one extra step, a moment where you have to consciously decide "yes, I'm pulling from savings for this." That single extra step is often enough to prevent the purchase, or at least to make it a conscious tradeoff instead of an invisible leak. This is the same mechanism as Chapter 1's "delete the decision point" — except here it's applied to withdrawals instead of deposits. A withdrawal that requires action is a withdrawal you'll actually think about.

This is worth dwelling on because it resolves an apparent contradiction in how this book uses the word "friction." Earlier chapters treat friction as the enemy — removing the friction between deciding to save and actually saving is the entire point of automation. This chapter treats friction as an ally, deliberately inserted between deciding to spend from savings and actually doing it. Both are the same principle applied in opposite directions: friction should sit wherever it favors the outcome you actually want. Zero friction on the deposit side, because you want deposits to happen without a fight. Real friction on the buffer or investment withdrawal side, because you want those withdrawals to happen only when you've genuinely decided they should. A system that gets this backward — friction on saving, none on spending savings — produces exactly the outcome most people are trying to escape. Getting it right, in both directions, is what this chapter's four-account structure is actually for.

The framework: the four-account minimum

A functional automatic system needs at minimum four accounts, each with one job:

1. Income/bills checking. Your paycheck lands here. Fixed costs — rent, utilities, insurance, minimum debt payments — get paid from here, ideally on autopay. This account's balance should stay close to a stable, boring number every month. If it's wildly fluctuating, something's misrouted.

2. Spending checking (or a dedicated card). A separate account or card that holds your discretionary/lifestyle money for the month, funded by one automatic transfer from the income account after fixed costs are covered. When this hits zero before the month ends, that's real information — not a crisis, just a signal the number needs adjusting next cycle. Keeping this separate from the bills account means a discretionary overspend can never accidentally eat into rent money, because rent money was never in the same place.

3. Buffer/emergency account. A separate, ideally slightly-harder-to-touch account (a different bank, no debit card attached, or a savings account with a brief transfer delay built in) that holds three to six months of fixed costs. This is what absorbs shocks — a car repair, a medical bill, a slow month — without derailing the rest of the system. The friction of having to transfer money *back* from this account, rather than it sitting in checking, is the entire point: it should require a real decision to touch.

4. Investment/long-term account. Money that's automatically swept here is meant to never come back to checking under normal circumstances. This is retirement accounts, brokerage accounts, or any account explicitly earmarked as long-horizon. Chapter 4 covers automating the contributions themselves; this chapter is just about making sure the account exists and is structurally separated from anything you can casually spend from.

Beyond these four, additional accounts for specific medium-term goals — a house down payment, a large planned purchase — follow the same logic: one account, one job, funded by its own automatic transfer, kept separate enough that it doesn't blur into general spending.

Worked example

Someone earning $5,500 a month sets up the following automatic flow, all triggered the day their paycheck lands: $3,600 stays in the bills checking account to cover fixed costs on autopay. $400 automatically transfers to a buffer account at a separate bank (no card, three-day external transfer delay). $300 automatically transfers to an investment account. $200 automatically transfers to a house-down-payment savings account. The remaining $1,000 automatically transfers to a spending account tied to their everyday debit card — and that account, not the paycheck-receiving one, is the only account they actually check day-to-day.

The result: the number they see most often — their spending account balance — is an *honest* number. It only ever reflects money that's actually available to spend, because everything else has already been physically relocated somewhere less convenient. There's no mental math required to figure out "how much of this can I actually spend." The account structure already did that math and physically enforced the answer.

Choosing which institutions actually hold these accounts

The account *types* matter less than the account *separation*, but a few practical choices make the separation hold up better in practice. The bills and spending accounts benefit from being at an institution with a strong everyday app, wide ATM or debit access, and no friction moving money in and out — because these are the accounts you interact with constantly, and any friction there works against you. The buffer account benefits from close to the opposite profile: an online-only bank or credit union, ideally one that isn't linked to a debit card at all, where moving money back out requires an explicit transfer that takes a day or more to land. That transfer delay isn't a flaw in the account — it's the entire feature. It's the friction that turns "I could just move this back to checking" into "let me actually think about whether I need to."

A high-yield savings account is generally the right vehicle for the buffer, since the money needs to stay liquid and safe rather than exposed to market swings — the buffer's job is to be there reliably during a crisis, not to grow aggressively. Medium-term goal accounts (the house down payment, the wedding, the planned large purchase within the next few years) usually belong in a similar low-volatility savings vehicle for the same reason: money you'll need on a known, relatively near-term date shouldn't be riding market volatility on the way there. Long-horizon investment accounts are the one category where the money should generally *not* sit in a savings account at all — cash sitting uninvested in a brokerage account isn't earning what it's meant to earn, which is precisely the failure mode Chapter 4 addresses directly.

Naming accounts so the architecture stays legible

A small, easy-to-skip step that prevents a surprising number of downstream mistakes: name each account by its job, not by its bank or a generic label. "Buffer — do not touch except real emergencies" is a far more effective label than "Savings 2," because the label itself becomes a piece of the friction system — every time you glance at your account list, the name reminds you what the money is for before you've made any decision about it. This matters most in the moment a temptation shows up: a clearly labeled account is harder to rationalize spending from than one that just looks like undifferentiated savings. It costs nothing to set up and it works every single time you open your banking app, which is more consistency than most financial advice can honestly claim.

A second worked example: renaming a drifted system back into shape

Someone with three years of automatic transfers already running discovers, during a review prompted by Chapter 9's audit habit, that their "savings" account has quietly become a catch-all — some of it is genuinely emergency reserve, some of it was meant for a car replacement, and some of it is just accumulated overflow with no assigned job. Rather than treating this as a failure of the system, they treat it as a structural gap: the account architecture never actually had a slot for "car replacement," so that money had nowhere correctly labeled to go and ended up blended into the general buffer instead.

The fix isn't complicated — it's opening one additional account, explicitly labeled and funded by its own small automatic transfer, and physically moving the car-replacement portion out of the general buffer into it. Once that's done, the buffer account's balance becomes an honest number again — a true read on actual emergency reserve, not emergency reserve blended with an unrelated future purchase. This is a useful pattern to keep in mind generally: when a single account starts serving more than one purpose, the fix is rarely to track the purposes more carefully in your head. It's to give each purpose its own account, the same way Chapter 1 argued in the first place.

How many accounts is too many

There's a natural instinct, once the logic of "one account, one job" clicks, to keep creating new accounts for every conceivable purpose — and it's worth naming the point where this stops helping and starts adding its own friction. An account structure with fifteen separate goal accounts, each funded by a tiny automatic transfer, becomes hard to monitor even during a quarterly review, and the administrative overhead of tracking that many destinations can itself become a reason the whole system gets abandoned. A reasonable ceiling for most situations: the four structural accounts from this chapter, plus one or two active medium-term goal accounts at a time. Once a goal account's purpose is fulfilled — the down payment is saved, the large purchase is made — close it or repurpose it for the next goal, rather than letting fulfilled-purpose accounts linger indefinitely and add clutter to a structure that's supposed to stay legible at a glance.

Digital-only banks versus traditional branches

Either type of institution can fill any of the four roles in this chapter's framework, and this book deliberately avoids recommending specific providers, since the competitive landscape shifts constantly. What matters structurally is less about digital-versus-branch and more about matching each account's friction level to its job: the bills and spending accounts benefit from fast, easy access regardless of format, while the buffer account benefits specifically from *some* deliberate friction, which digital-only banks without physical branches or attached debit cards often provide naturally, simply because there's no branch to walk into and no card to tap. If your buffer sits at a traditional bank with a linked debit card and instant mobile transfers, the friction this chapter relies on doesn't really exist — worth checking specifically for that gap when you're first setting the account up, since it's a structural property of the account, not a matter of self-discipline once it's already open.

Setting up the actual transfers: a practical sequence

Translating this chapter's framework into a working system generally follows a specific order, worth laying out explicitly rather than leaving implicit. First, open whichever of the four account types you don't already have, choosing institutions deliberately per the friction considerations above rather than defaulting to whatever's most convenient. Second, confirm your exact paycheck landing date or dates, since every automatic transfer in this system needs to be timed against that date rather than an arbitrary calendar day. Third, set up the transfers themselves in a specific order: fixed-cost autopay from the bills account first (since a missed bill payment carries real consequences), then the pay-yourself-first transfers to buffer, goal, and investment accounts, then the transfer to the spending account last, sized to whatever remains. Fourth, let one full paycheck cycle run before making any adjustments, so you're reacting to what actually happened rather than a prediction of what might happen. Fifth, review after that first cycle and adjust amounts if needed — a first attempt at these numbers is a hypothesis, not a permanent commitment, and Chapter 9's quarterly review habit is where ongoing refinement happens from that point forward.

This sequencing matters because setting up transfers in the wrong order — for instance, setting the spending account amount first and hoping the pay-yourself-first transfers fit around whatever's left — inverts the entire logic of this book. The spending account should always be the residual, sized by what's left after the more important allocations, never the other way around.

Joint accounts, individual accounts, and the household version of this architecture

Couples merging finances entirely into joint accounts and couples keeping everything fully separate both run into predictable friction points, and the four-account framework in this chapter adapts cleanly to a middle structure that avoids both. A joint bills account, funded by each partner's proportional contribution (proportional to income, not necessarily an even split, which better matches genuine shared burden when incomes differ) handles shared fixed costs. A joint or individually-held buffer account, agreed on jointly even if held in one partner's name for practical reasons, serves the household's shared emergency needs. Individual spending accounts, one per partner, each funded by an agreed amount, preserve a meaningful degree of individual financial autonomy — a genuinely useful design choice, since forcing every discretionary dollar through a shared account tends to generate friction over small purchases that a joint household budget was never really meant to litigate individually. Joint or individual investment accounts can go either way depending on the couple's preference and legal/tax considerations specific to their situation, which is genuinely outside the scope of a book focused on mechanics rather than individual circumstances.

The core principle doesn't change across any of these configurations: every dollar needs a named job and a structural home that matches that job, whether the household is running one big shared pool or several coordinated individual ones. What changes is simply how many parallel copies of the four-account structure exist and how the proportional funding across them is decided — a conversation worth having explicitly and revisiting at the same quarterly cadence as everything else in this book, rather than assumed to be permanently settled the first time it comes up.

Why account separation outperforms tracking software

A reasonable question at this point: couldn't all of this be accomplished with a single account and good budgeting software that tracks categories and labels internally, rather than physically separating the money into different accounts? Some software genuinely does a good job of *tracking* this kind of separation. But tracking and structural separation solve different problems, and this book cares specifically about the second one. Software that shows you "$800 of this $4,000 balance is earmarked for savings" is still showing you a single spendable number that happens to have a label attached — and per Chapter 1's core mechanism, a visible, accessible balance reads as spendable regardless of the label sitting next to it. The friction that makes physical account separation effective isn't about visibility or tracking accuracy; it's about the number of deliberate steps between "I want to spend this" and "I've spent this." A label reduces that number of steps to zero. A separate account, especially one at a different institution without a linked card, keeps that number meaningfully above zero. Software is an excellent tool for monitoring a system that's already structurally sound. It's a poor substitute for the structural separation itself.

The architecture as the foundation every later chapter builds on

It's worth being explicit that this chapter isn't one option among several equally valid approaches covered later in the book — it's the physical foundation every other chapter assumes already exists. The pay-yourself-first percentage from Chapter 2 needs somewhere structurally protected to land. The investment automation in Chapter 4 needs a dedicated account separate from anything spendable. The variable-income structure in Chapter 6 is, at its core, an extension of this same account-separation logic applied to an income-smoothing problem rather than a spending problem. The flex fund in Chapter 8 is simply another named, separated account with its own defined job. If you build only one piece of this book's system before setting the rest aside for later, this is the piece to build first — not because the other mechanics matter less, but because none of them have anywhere correct to attach until this architecture exists underneath them.

Migrating an existing tangle of accounts into this structure

Very few readers are starting from a completely blank slate — most already have some collection of accounts, opened at various points for various reasons, that don't cleanly map onto this chapter's four-account framework. Migrating an existing tangle doesn't require closing everything and starting over; it requires auditing what exists against the four roles this chapter defines (bills, spending, buffer, investment) and identifying which existing accounts can be repurposed, which need to be opened fresh, and which serve no clear ongoing purpose and can be closed once their balance is moved somewhere with an actual job. Do this migration in one sitting rather than piecemeal over months — a half-migrated system, with some money following the new structure and some still sitting in the old undifferentiated arrangement, tends to confuse rather than clarify, since it reintroduces exactly the blurred-purpose problem this chapter exists to solve. A single afternoon spent consolidating and relabeling existing accounts into their correct roles is worth far more than a gradual drift toward the same structure over an extended, half-committed period.

What to do with old, dormant, or forgotten accounts

Part of a migration audit typically turns up accounts that don't map cleanly onto any of the four roles at all — an old checking account from a previous bank, kept open out of inertia; a savings account opened years ago for a goal that's since changed or been abandoned; a small forgotten balance sitting somewhere with no clear function. These deserve a direct decision rather than being left in limbo indefinitely: either fold the balance into one of the four structural accounts where it actually belongs, or close the account outright if it's serving no purpose. Dormant accounts carry a quiet cost beyond the inconvenience of tracking them — they're one more surface where a fee could silently apply, one more login to maintain, one more place a balance can sit unassigned and therefore, per this book's core argument, effectively unprotected. A clean four-account structure with nothing extra hanging off it is easier to monitor at each quarterly review than the same structure with three or four legacy accounts still lingering in the background, unexamined.

Chapter 4 — Automating the Investment Contribution

Why "I'll Invest What's Left Over" Guarantees You Won't

Investing suffers from the exact same sequencing problem as saving, with one added layer: it also competes against the temptation to time the market, wait for a "better" entry point, or second-guess a contribution during a downturn. Left to manual decisions, investing doesn't just get deprioritized behind spending — it gets deprioritized behind your own anxiety about *when* to do it. Automation solves both problems at once, because an automatic contribution doesn't check the news before it executes.

This chapter treats investment contributions as an extension of the pay-yourself-first mechanic from Chapter 2, applied specifically to the portion of your automated savings that's meant to grow over decades rather than sit as a buffer.

It's worth being clear about the boundary between what this chapter covers and what it deliberately leaves alone. This is not a chapter about which specific investments to choose, how to build an allocation, or how to think about risk tolerance — those are real, important questions, but they're portfolio-construction questions, not automation-mechanics questions, and they depend heavily on individual circumstances this book can't responsibly generalize about. What this chapter covers is narrower and, for the purposes of this book, more foundational: once you've decided what to invest in, how do you make sure the decision to actually contribute to it, consistently, keeps happening without needing to be re-made every month. That's a mechanics question, and it has a concrete, repeatable answer regardless of which specific investments sit on the other end of the automated transfer.

What's actually happening

Two separate failure modes show up when investing isn't automated. The first is the same erosion problem from earlier chapters: "I'll invest the extra money at the end of the month" almost never happens, because there's rarely extra money left by the time the end of the month arrives — it's been absorbed by convenience spending along the way. The second is specific to investing: even people who do have money set aside for it often hesitate at the moment of actually placing the trade, waiting for a dip, a correction, better news, a clearer signal. That hesitation, repeated monthly, quietly turns into months or years of contributions that never actually happen, even though the money was technically "there."

Automating the contribution removes both failure modes at once. If the transfer and purchase execute on a schedule regardless of what the market did last week, there's no month where "extra money" needs to survive to the end, and there's no moment where a decision about market timing gets to intervene. The contribution simply happens, the same way a mortgage payment happens, whether or not you feel good about it that particular week.

The mortgage comparison is worth sitting with for a moment, because it captures exactly what this chapter is asking you to build. Nobody debates, month to month, whether it's a good time to make a mortgage payment based on how the housing market is performing that week — the payment is simply due, on a schedule, regardless of sentiment. Investment contributions, left unautomated, get treated completely differently: as a discretionary decision, re-litigated every single month, subject to mood, news cycles, and market anxiety in a way a fixed mortgage payment never is. This chapter's entire mechanic is about closing that gap — treating the investment contribution with the same structural non-negotiability as a bill, rather than as a discretionary choice that has to win a fresh argument against hesitation every single time it comes due.

The framework: what to automate, and in what order

1. Automate the transfer, then automate the purchase. Two separate steps, both automatable independently. Most retirement accounts (employer-sponsored plans, for instance) automate both by default through payroll deduction — the money never even touches your checking account. For a taxable brokerage account, you typically need to set up both pieces yourself: an automatic transfer from checking to the brokerage on a schedule, and a recurring automatic purchase of your chosen investments once the cash lands. Leaving the second step manual reintroduces exactly the hesitation problem this chapter is trying to eliminate — cash sitting in a brokerage account, uninvested, waiting for a "good time" that never quite arrives.

2. Order your accounts by structural benefit before amount. Before deciding how much goes where, decide the order accounts get funded in. A common structural order — not a universal rule, but a reasonable default to test against your own situation — is: first, any employer retirement match up to the full match amount (this is close to a guaranteed return you'd otherwise leave on the table); second, any high-interest debt that's costing more than a reasonable expected investment return; third, tax-advantaged retirement accounts up to their limits; fourth, taxable investment accounts for anything beyond that. Automate contributions in that order so the highest-value dollars are always funded first, regardless of how the month goes.

3. Pick a schedule that matches your pay, not the calendar. Contributions timed to land the same day your paycheck does — rather than a fixed calendar date that might precede payday — avoid the awkward situation where an automatic withdrawal fires before the money to cover it has arrived.

4. Choose a fixed contribution, not a "whatever's available" percentage of a fluctuating account. The contribution amount should be a fixed dollar figure (or, for variable income, a fixed percentage set up per Chapter 6's mechanics) decided in advance — not something that adjusts based on your checking account balance at the moment the transfer fires. A fixed number removes the temptation to quietly lower it during a month that feels tight, which is exactly the kind of manual override this whole system is designed to avoid needing.

Worked example

Someone with access to an employer retirement plan that matches contributions up to 4% of salary sets their payroll deduction to exactly 4% — full match captured automatically, no decision required each paycheck. They then set up a second, separate automatic transfer of $300 a month from checking to a taxable brokerage account, timed to land two days after payday. Inside the brokerage account, they set a recurring automatic purchase of a small number of diversified funds for the same day the transfer clears, so the cash never sits uninvested waiting for a "better entry point."

Across a year, this produces a guaranteed 4% employer-matched retirement contribution plus $3,600 invested in the brokerage account — all without a single manual trade, and without a single month where market anxiety got the chance to delay a purchase. The amount isn't dramatic by itself. What matters is that it happened in every single month, including the ones where the news was bad and the instinct to wait would have been strongest.

Rebalancing without turning it back into a manual decision

Contributions aren't the only investing task that suffers when it's left manual — rebalancing, the periodic process of bringing your actual asset mix back in line with your intended one after markets move it out of alignment, has the exact same failure pattern. Left as a "someday" task, it tends to either never happen at all, or happen reactively during a downturn, which is close to the worst possible timing: rebalancing during a period of fear tends to mean selling what's fallen and buying what's held up, the opposite of the discipline rebalancing is supposed to enforce.

Many retirement accounts and some brokerage platforms offer automatic rebalancing on a fixed schedule — quarterly or annually — that brings your holdings back to a target allocation without requiring a manual trade each time. Where that feature exists, turning it on removes rebalancing from the list of things that depend on you remembering, or worse, depend on you having the emotional steadiness to do it correctly during a stressful market. Where it doesn't exist, the fallback is the same pattern used throughout this book: a fixed calendar trigger — the same quarterly review from Chapter 9 is a natural place to attach it — rather than a vague intention to "check on it sometime."

What to do when your employer plan limits automation

Not every employer-sponsored retirement plan offers full automation flexibility — some restrict how often you can change your contribution percentage, some don't offer automatic rebalancing, and some have a limited fund menu that doesn't perfectly match what you'd choose on an open platform.

None of this breaks the mechanic; it just means the *first* automated step (the payroll deduction itself, up to at least the full employer match) still captures the highest-value piece automatically, and any further customization can happen through a second, separate account you have full control over — the taxable brokerage account in the worked example above, or an individual retirement account outside the employer plan, depending on what's available and appropriate for your situation. The goal isn't to find one account that does everything perfectly. It's to make sure every dollar you intend to invest has *some* automated home, even if that means splitting the job across two accounts instead of one.

A second worked example: catching up after a late start

Someone in their late thirties with no prior retirement contributions decides to start now rather than treating the late start as a reason to wait for a "better" moment — a decision that, per Chapter 1's core argument, would likely never actually arrive on its own. They set their employer plan's payroll deduction to the maximum they can sustain against a bad-month test (per Chapter 2's method), which comes out to 9% of salary, immediately capturing a 4% employer match on top of it. They pair this with a modest $150 monthly automatic transfer into a separate account for a period they expect to be able to increase contributions further, once other financial goals — an existing debt payoff, in this case — are further along.

The point of this example isn't the specific percentage; it's that automating an imperfect, currently-achievable contribution today outperforms waiting to automate a theoretically better one at some unspecified future point. A 9% automated contribution that starts now and compounds for the next two decades will, in almost every realistic scenario, outperform a hypothetical 15% contribution that gets endlessly postponed until "things settle down." The system doesn't need to be optimal on day one. It needs to exist on day one, and Chapter 7's escalation mechanic handles making it better over time.

Vesting schedules and what "automatic" means when the employer is also involved

Some employer retirement matches vest over a period of time rather than becoming fully yours the moment they're contributed — meaning if you leave the job before a certain point, some or all of the matched portion (not your own contributions, which are always yours) may not transfer with you. This doesn't change the automation logic in this chapter, but it's worth checking your specific plan's vesting schedule as part of setting the contribution up, since it affects how you think about the value of that match if a job change is realistically on the horizon. The employer match remains worth automating and capturing regardless — a partially or fully vested match is still better than no match — but understanding the vesting terms prevents an unpleasant surprise if you leave earlier than expected and discover part of what you assumed was already yours wasn't.

When the contribution amount and the tax-advantaged limit don't line up

Tax-advantaged retirement accounts typically carry an annual contribution limit set by the relevant tax authority, and these limits are adjusted periodically — which is exactly why this book avoids stating a specific figure that would be stale within a year or two. What matters mechanically is building your automated contribution with the current limit in mind, so a fixed monthly transfer doesn't either fall meaningfully short of what you're allowed to contribute (leaving tax-advantaged room unused) or, less commonly, attempt to exceed it (which most platforms will simply reject or cap automatically, but is worth avoiding by design rather than relying on the platform to catch). A brief annual check — a natural pairing with the yearly portion of your quarterly review cycle — to confirm your automated contribution rate still makes sense against the current limit and your current income keeps this detail from silently drifting out of alignment over time.

Dollar-cost averaging as an automatic side effect, not a separate strategy

You'll sometimes see dollar-cost averaging discussed as though it were a deliberate market-timing strategy someone chooses to adopt. In the context of this book, it isn't a separate decision at all — it's simply the natural consequence of automating a fixed contribution on a fixed schedule, regardless of price, which is exactly what Chapter 2's pay-yourself-first mechanic already produces once it's pointed at an investment account. There's no additional step required to "start dollar-cost averaging"; if your investment contributions are already automated on a recurring schedule, you're already doing it, by construction. Naming this explicitly matters because it removes a subtle source of hesitation: the recurring worry, in a down market, about whether now is a bad time to be buying. Under a fixed automated schedule, "now" was never a decision you had to make — the schedule made it in advance, on a day when the market's mood wasn't a consideration at all, which is precisely the point.

A note on employer plan default investments

When a retirement account is opened through payroll enrollment, many plans place new contributions into a default investment option automatically, simply so the money isn't left uninvested while a decision gets made. This default is usually a reasonable, broadly diversified starting point, but it's worth deliberately confirming it matches your actual intended allocation rather than assuming it does — a default is a fallback for people who haven't made an active choice, not necessarily the choice you would have made yourself. This is a one-time check to make during initial setup, not a recurring task; once your allocation is deliberately chosen and automation is layered on top of it, per this chapter's framework, it should require no further manual attention beyond the periodic rebalancing check described earlier.

Automating around a windfall investment decision

Not every investment contribution arrives as a small, regular paycheck deduction — a bonus, an inheritance, the proceeds from selling a large asset, or any other lump sum presents a different version of the automation challenge, since there's no recurring schedule to plug it into. The instinct with a large lump sum is often to treat the investing decision as a single, high-stakes, one-time choice — which reintroduces exactly the hesitation and timing anxiety this chapter's automated recurring contributions are designed to avoid. A workable middle path: rather than either investing the entire lump sum at once (which can feel emotionally risky, even though it's often the mathematically reasonable choice for genuinely long-horizon money) or leaving it in cash indefinitely while searching for a "better time" (which tends to become permanent, per Chapter

1's core argument), set up a short, automatic schedule that invests the lump sum in several equal installments over a matter of weeks or a few months. This isn't a claim about which approach produces a better long-run return — reasonable arguments exist on both sides, and this book isn't the place to adjudicate them — it's a claim about which approach is more likely to actually get executed rather than delayed indefinitely by exactly the kind of manual, emotionally loaded decision this book exists to design around.

Why market conditions shouldn't change the automation itself

A recurring temptation, once a downturn or a period of unusual volatility hits, is to manually pause automated investment contributions "until things stabilize." This is worth naming directly as a mistake, and one of the most costly ones this book covers, because it inverts the entire logic dollar-cost averaging depends on. A fixed contribution buys more shares when prices are lower and fewer when prices are higher, automatically, without requiring you to correctly judge which is which in the moment — which is valuable specifically because nobody, including professional investors, reliably identifies market bottoms or tops in real time. Pausing contributions during a downturn means skipping exactly the purchases that a purely mechanical, unemotional system would have made at relatively favorable prices, replaced by a judgment call made under the emotional pressure of watching account values fall — precisely the condition Chapter 1 identified as the worst possible state for making a good financial decision. The entire value of automating this contribution in the first place was to remove that judgment call. Reintroducing it selectively, only during the exact periods when judgment is most likely to be clouded, defeats the purpose more thoroughly than never having automated the contribution at all.

The specific difference between automating and forgetting

There's a distinction worth drawing precisely, because it separates this chapter's advice from a common misreading of it: automating an investment contribution means removing the *decision* about whether to invest, not removing your *awareness* of the account entirely. Chapter 9's quarterly review still applies fully to investment accounts — confirming contributions are actually landing and actually being invested rather than sitting as cash, confirming the allocation still matches your intentions, confirming any employer match hasn't quietly changed its terms. "Automatic" describes the mechanism that executes the contribution and the purchase. It doesn't describe a policy of never looking at the account again. The two get conflated often enough that it's worth stating the boundary explicitly: automate the execution, but keep the periodic, low-frequency oversight that catches drift, exactly as every other automated piece of this book's system requires.

Automating across multiple investment accounts without losing track

Once more than one investment account is running — an employer plan, a taxable brokerage, perhaps an account earmarked for a specific medium-term goal — it becomes easy to lose a clear sense of the whole picture, since each account shows its own automation running correctly in isolation without any single view of how they add up together. A simple fix, worth setting up once and revisiting at each quarterly review: a single summary line, even a basic note or spreadsheet row, listing every automated investment contribution across every account, its amount, its frequency, and its purpose. This isn't meant to replace the automation itself — each account keeps running independently exactly as designed — it's meant to give you, at a glance, the one piece of visibility automation deliberately removes from day-to-day life: a sense of the total picture, checked occasionally rather than tracked constantly, so you can confirm the pieces are still adding up to something coherent rather than several disconnected automations that happen to share your name.

Starting small when the numbers feel intimidating

It's worth addressing directly a hesitation that keeps some readers from starting this chapter's automation at all: the sense that investing is something you do once you have a substantial amount to invest, or once you understand markets more thoroughly, rather than something you begin with a small, automatic, recurring amount and grow into over time. This gets the sequencing backward. The mechanics in this chapter work identically whether the recurring contribution is a modest amount or a substantial one — the account still needs to be opened, the transfer still needs to be scheduled, the purchase still needs to be automated so cash doesn't sit idle. A small contribution automated today, and left running, builds both the habit and the account balance simultaneously, and the escalation mechanics from Chapter 7 exist specifically to grow that starting contribution over time as circumstances allow. Waiting to begin until the contribution amount feels sufficiently impressive is simply another version of the "waiting for the right moment" trap covered in Chapter 1 — and it costs the exact years of compounding this chapter's entire mechanic depends on to be worth building in the first place.

Chapter 5 — The Subscription and Recurring-Cost Audit

Why Recurring Costs Are the Leak Automation Doesn't Catch on Its Own

Everything built so far automates the *good* side of the ledger — money moving toward savings and investing before you can spend it. But automation cuts both ways: recurring subscriptions and services are automatically charging you every month whether you use them or not, with the same "you never see the decision point" mechanic working against you instead of for you. A subscription doesn't ask permission each month. It just charges the card and continues until someone actively stops it.

This chapter builds a system for finding and killing those leaks — and then, critically, for negotiating down the recurring costs that are legitimate and worth keeping — on a repeating schedule, rather than as a one-time cleanup that quietly goes stale within a year.

It's worth noting up front why this chapter sits between the investment automation of Chapter 4 and the variable-income mechanics of Chapter 6 rather than earlier in the book, closer to the account-architecture chapter it might seem to pair with most naturally. The reason is sequencing: a subscription audit performed before the pay-yourself-first and investment automation are in place tends to produce recovered money with nowhere defined to go, which per Chapter 1's core mechanic means it quietly gets reabsorbed into ordinary spending rather than compounding anywhere. Performed after those earlier mechanics are running, the same audit's recovered dollars have an obvious, pre-built destination waiting for them — which is exactly the pattern this chapter's own worked example demonstrates.

This placement also means the audit habit is being introduced at the point in the book where every other automated piece is already live, which is deliberate: by Chapter 5, you've already built the account architecture, the pay-yourself-first transfer, and the investment contribution, so this chapter isn't asking you to build a new destination for recovered money — it's asking you to redirect money into destinations that already exist and are already running. That's a meaningfully smaller ask than it would be if this chapter came first, before any of that infrastructure existed to receive the results.

What's actually happening

Recurring charges benefit from the exact same invisibility that Chapter 1 identified as the core problem with unstructured spending: a $12.99 charge that hits your card automatically every month never has to survive a spending decision, because there is no decision — it just happens. Individually, these charges look trivial. Collectively, across streaming services, apps, memberships, and software trials that were never canceled, they routinely add up to a meaningful chunk of monthly spending that nobody consciously chose to keep paying for.

The second failure mode is separate from forgotten subscriptions: legitimate, actively-used recurring costs — insurance premiums, phone plans, internet service — that were priced correctly when you signed up and have quietly crept upward since, through renewal-cycle price increases that arrive as a line-item change nobody flags for review. These aren't subscriptions to cancel; they're costs to periodically renegotiate, and most people never do, because there's no natural trigger that reminds them to.

The framework: audit, cut, negotiate, recur

1. Pull every recurring charge from the last twelve months, not just what you remember. Memory is unreliable here by design — the whole reason these charges are a problem is that they're invisible. Go through actual statements (most banking apps now flag recurring transactions automatically) rather than relying on a mental list, which will systematically miss anything you've stopped noticing.

2. Sort into three categories: cancel, downgrade, negotiate. *Cancel* is anything unused or barely used — the trial that was supposed to be temporary, the app you opened twice. *Downgrade* is anything you use but not at the tier you're paying for — a subscription tier with features you don't touch. *Negotiate* is legitimate, actively-used costs that are priced above what's currently available, where a phone call or chat message can often bring the price back down, especially for services with competitive alternatives (insurance, phone plans, internet, and similar recurring contracts are the most common candidates).

3. Build a negotiation script you can reuse, not one you improvise each time. A workable version: state that you're reviewing your account and considering switching providers, ask directly whether there's a lower rate, promotion, or loyalty discount available, and if the answer is no, ask to be transferred to a retention or cancellation department — which frequently has more authority to offer a better rate than a first-line representative does. This isn't a trick; it's simply asking the question most people never ask, to the department actually authorized to answer it.

4. Automate the audit itself, on a fixed calendar trigger, not a "when I remember" basis. Set a recurring calendar reminder — quarterly is a reasonable cadence — to run this exact process again. The audit doesn't need to be automated in the sense of requiring no human involvement (negotiation calls still need a person), but the *trigger* to do it should be automatic, so it doesn't depend on you noticing the leak has crept back.

Worked example

A quarterly audit turns up four streaming subscriptions where only two are actually watched, a fitness app trial that auto-converted to a paid plan eight months ago and was never used again, and a phone plan that's crept up through two renewal cycles without any change in service. Canceling the two unused streaming services and the forgotten fitness app saves roughly $34 a month. A ten-minute call to the phone provider, using the reusable negotiation script above and asking specifically to be transferred to the retention department, brings the monthly phone bill down by $20.

That's $54 a month, $648 a year, recovered without a single change to lifestyle or spending behavior — nothing was given up, because nothing was actually being used or fairly priced in the first place. Routed automatically into the investment account from Chapter 4 rather than absorbed back into discretionary spending, that recovered $54 becomes part of the same compounding system as every other automated dollar. The audit itself takes under an hour, four times a year — a small, scheduled cost in exchange for a leak that would otherwise run indefinitely, invisibly, for years.

Annual charges are the ones that hide best

Monthly subscriptions are relatively easy to spot on a statement, because they show up twelve times a year. Annual charges — a domain renewal, a once-a-year software license, a membership billed on its signup anniversary rather than a predictable calendar date — are far easier to miss, precisely because they only appear once, on a date that isn't obviously tied to anything else happening that month. A single unexpected annual charge often gets written off as a one-time anomaly rather than recognized as the same recurring cost it actually is, simply because a year has passed since the last time it appeared and the pattern isn't obvious in the moment.

The fix is to extend the audit window beyond the most recent month or two, and specifically look across a full twelve months of statements at least once during your quarterly review cycle, flagging anything that only appears once but is clearly tied to a renewal date rather than a genuine one-off purchase. Many of these carry the steepest effective price increases too, since annual renewal pricing tends to creep upward with less scrutiny than a monthly charge that a customer sees, and has the chance to react to, far more often.

Negotiating insurance specifically

Insurance — auto, renters, homeowners, and similar recurring policies — deserves a slightly different version of the negotiation script from earlier in this chapter, because unlike a streaming subscription, canceling outright usually isn't the right move; the coverage is generally still needed. The better lever is comparison: gathering a current quote or two from competing providers before making the call, and using that concrete number as the anchor for the conversation, rather than a vague request for "a better rate." A specific competing quote in hand is a fundamentally different conversation than a general ask — it gives the representative something concrete to match or beat, rather than an open-ended request they have no particular incentive to act on.

This is also a case where the pre-planned, automatic *trigger* matters more than the negotiation itself: insurance rates tend to creep upward gradually at each renewal, in small enough increments that any single increase rarely feels worth contesting.

Tying a review specifically to each policy's renewal date — a calendar reminder set the moment you get the renewal notice, not a general quarterly sweep that might miss the narrow window where switching or renegotiating is easiest — catches the increase at the one point in the year it's actually actionable.

A second worked example: comparing before calling

Ahead of an auto insurance renewal notice, someone spends fifteen minutes getting two comparison quotes from other providers before their current policy auto-renews. Both quotes come in noticeably lower than the renewal price for equivalent coverage. Rather than switching immediately, they call their current provider first, mention the renewal notice, state plainly that they've received lower quotes elsewhere for the same coverage, and ask whether the current provider can match or beat either one. The representative applies a loyalty discount and a bundling adjustment that brings the renewal price down to roughly match the better of the two competing quotes.

The outcome — a lower premium, no need to actually switch providers, no lapse in coverage during a transition —

required no special negotiating skill beyond having a specific number to anchor the conversation to and asking the question directly. Most of the value in this interaction came from the automated trigger (the calendar reminder tied to the renewal date) ensuring the conversation happened at all, at the one point in the year it could actually change anything. Left to happen "whenever it comes to mind," this conversation, like most of the ones in this book, simply wouldn't have happened.

Building a simple recurring-cost inventory

The audit process described earlier in this chapter works best when it's written down somewhere durable, rather than re-derived from memory each quarter. A simple inventory — a spreadsheet or even a plain document — listing every recurring charge, its amount, its billing frequency, its renewal or anniversary date, and the date you last reviewed it, turns a vague "I should look into subscriptions sometime" into a concrete, repeatable checklist. Each quarterly review becomes a matter of working down an existing list and updating it, rather than starting from scratch trying to remember what you're even paying for. This is a small piece of infrastructure, but it's the same principle as everything else in this book: a process that depends on memory alone will eventually fail; a process backed by a persistent, low-effort record survives far longer.

Negotiating costs tied to a freelance business or side income

If you run a freelance business or side income stream (which connects directly to Chapter 6), the recurring-cost audit applies just as much to business expenses as to personal ones — software subscriptions, tool licenses, payment processing fees, and similar recurring business costs are just as prone to the same forgotten-trial and creeping-renewal-price patterns as personal subscriptions, and are often reviewed even less often, since business expenses can feel like a fixed cost of doing business rather than something worth periodically challenging. The same three-category sort — cancel, downgrade, negotiate — and the same quarterly trigger apply without modification. Business software vendors in particular are often more willing to negotiate pricing than consumer subscription services are, especially for annual commitments or when a genuine competing option is mentioned, simply because the value of retaining a paying business customer tends to be higher to the vendor than retaining an individual consumer subscriber.

The psychological trap of "it's only a few dollars"

A single subscription at a few dollars a month rarely feels worth the effort of canceling — the mental math makes the time spent seem disproportionate to the savings gained. This reasoning is accurate for any one subscription in isolation and misleading for the category as a whole, because the "it's only a few dollars" thought applies independently to every individual charge, and a household running eight or ten small unused or overpriced recurring costs is running that same undervalued reasoning eight or ten times simultaneously. The fix isn't to evaluate each charge's cancellation-worthiness in isolation — it's to evaluate the audit as a single batched task covering the full list at once, where the cumulative recovered amount is what gets weighed against the (also cumulative, but still modest) time spent, rather than comparing one $8 charge against the ten minutes it would take to cancel it. Framed as a single quarterly task with a real total attached, rather than a series of individually unconvincing micro-decisions, the audit consistently proves worth doing — which is exactly why it belongs on a fixed calendar trigger rather than left to case-by-case judgment.

What to do when a cancellation gets actively resisted

Some subscription services make cancellation deliberately difficult — a phone call required instead of a self-serve option, a retention offer pushed hard before the cancellation is processed, a multi-step confirmation flow clearly designed to cause drop-off. Knowing this in advance changes the audit from a mild inconvenience into a genuinely useful piece of information: services that make cancellation this difficult are often signaling, structurally, that voluntary retention on the merits is not working, which is itself a data point worth remembering the next time that category of service is being chosen or renewed. Practically, the move is simply to expect and push through the friction rather than let it discourage the cancellation attempt in the moment — state the cancellation request plainly and repeat it if a retention offer is presented that doesn't genuinely serve you, rather than accepting a partial discount on a service you'd already decided you don't need.

Preventing new leaks, not just fixing existing ones

Everything so far in this chapter addresses cleanup — finding and eliminating leaks that already exist. It's worth pairing that with a small upstream habit that reduces how many new leaks accumulate between audits in the first place: before starting any new subscription or free trial, set a calendar reminder a few days before the trial converts to paid, or before the first renewal date on a new subscription, specifically to decide, deliberately, whether to keep it. This flips the default from "stays active until someone notices and cancels it" to "requires an active, conscious choice to continue" — the same friction-reversal principle from Chapter 1, applied specifically to the moment a new recurring cost is created rather than waiting to catch it later in a quarterly sweep. A subscription that survives one of these deliberate check-ins is a subscription you've actually chosen, rather than one that simply hasn't been noticed yet.

Redirecting recovered money instead of letting it re-absorb

An audit that recovers $50 a month and simply lets that $50 sit unassigned in the checking account accomplishes less than it appears to, because unassigned money in a checking account is exactly the condition Chapter 1 identified as the default path toward quiet, convenience-driven spending. The audit's actual value is only fully captured when the recovered amount is immediately redirected somewhere with a defined job — increasing the pay-yourself-first transfer from Chapter 2 by the recovered amount, funding the buffer if it isn't yet full, or adding to the investment contribution from Chapter 4. Treat every successful cancellation or negotiation as an automatic trigger in its own right: the moment a recurring cost is eliminated or reduced, immediately update the relevant automatic transfer to capture the difference, in the same sitting, before the freed-up amount has a chance to quietly become part of an inflated "available" balance that eventually gets absorbed into ordinary spending without ever being a deliberate choice.

Treating the audit as a genuinely enjoyable task, not a chore

Framing matters more than it might seem for a task that's easy to indefinitely postpone. An audit approached as "finding money you're already earning that's currently being wasted" tends to actually get done, quarter after quarter, in a way that an audit approached as "another financial chore to feel guilty about avoiding" doesn't. This isn't a trivial point about mindset layered awkwardly onto an otherwise mechanical book — it's a practical observation about which framing survives contact with a busy quarter. A recurring task people find at least mildly satisfying gets protected time on a calendar far more reliably than one they dread. Treat each quarterly audit as a short scavenger hunt with a real, countable prize at the end — the specific dollar figure recovered that quarter — rather than an obligation, and the habit tends to outlast the ones approached with resigned duty instead.

Chapter 6 — Automating the System on Variable Income

Why Fixed-Dollar Automation Breaks the First Month Income Drops

Everything in this book so far assumes a predictable paycheck landing on a predictable schedule. If you freelance, run a business, work commission-based sales, or otherwise have income that swings from month to month, a fixed-dollar automatic transfer is a liability, not a solution — it'll either fire during a lean month and force an overdraft or an emergency-fund raid, or it'll be set conservatively low enough to survive lean months and leave real money on the table during strong ones.

This chapter adapts everything built in Chapters 1 through 5 for variable income, without abandoning the core principle: the good decision still needs to be automatic, it just can't be pegged to a fixed dollar amount tied to a calendar date.

If you have a stable paycheck and this chapter genuinely doesn't apply to you, it's still worth reading rather than skipping outright, for a reason unrelated to your own current situation:

careers change. A salaried role today can become a consulting arrangement, a business, or a portfolio of freelance income at some future point, often without much advance warning, and the mechanics in this chapter are the ones that situation will call for whenever it arrives. Understanding the two-layer structure now, even as a purely theoretical exercise, means you won't be building it from scratch under time pressure if and when your own income pattern actually shifts.

What's actually happening

Variable income breaks fixed-transfer automation in a specific, predictable way: the system doesn't know, in advance, whether this month's income will cover a fixed transfer amount plus fixed costs. A $600 automatic transfer that works fine on a $6,000 month becomes a real problem on a $2,800 month. The instinct, at that point, is usually to disable automation altogether and go back to manual, ad hoc saving — which reintroduces every failure mode from Chapter 1 and generally means saving quietly drops toward zero, exactly the outcome automation was meant to prevent.

This is worth naming as its own specific trap, distinct from the general case covered in Chapter 1: it's not that variable-income earners are less capable of sticking to a system, it's that the specific mechanic — a fixed dollar amount on a fixed date — was simply built for a different kind of income than the one they actually have. Applying a salaried template to variable income isn't a matter of trying harder to make it work; it's a mismatch between the tool and the problem, the same way a wrench doesn't fail to turn a bolt because you weren't gripping it firmly enough — it fails because it's the wrong size for that particular bolt. This chapter exists to build the correctly sized tool, not to ask variable-income earners to somehow force the salaried version to fit.

The actual fix isn't to abandon automation for variable income — it's to change what triggers it. Instead of a fixed amount on a fixed date, the trigger becomes a percentage applied to income *as it arrives*, combined with a buffer account that exists specifically to convert irregular income into a regular, predictable paycheck for the rest of the system to work against.

The framework: the two-layer variable-income system

Layer one — the income smoothing account. All variable income, regardless of source or amount, lands in a single dedicated account first — not the bills or spending accounts. This account's only job is to receive irregular deposits. From there, a fixed, self-paid "salary" transfers out to the bills and spending accounts on a regular schedule (weekly or monthly), set at a conservative level based on your lowest realistic income months, not your average or best ones. This converts unpredictable income into the exact predictable paycheck every mechanic in Chapters 1 through 5 was built around — once the money reaches the bills and spending accounts, the rest of the system doesn't need to know or care that the income was irregular in the first place.

Layer two — percentage-based allocation at the point of deposit, not the point of self-payment. Rather than applying pay-yourself-first percentages to the smoothed "salary," apply a percentage split the moment income actually lands in the smoothing account — before it's even distributed as salary. A reasonable structure: an immediate percentage (say, 25-30%) automatically routed out of every incoming deposit to cover taxes (self-employed and freelance income typically isn't withheld the way payroll income is, and this is the single most common point of failure in variable-income systems — treat the tax set-aside as non-negotiable and automatic, not an end-of-year scramble), a further percentage to the buffer/emergency account until it's fully funded, and the remainder feeding the self-paid salary described in layer one. During unusually strong months, an extra step can route a portion of anything above your typical income level directly to investing, rather than letting a single good month quietly raise your baseline spending — a variable-income-specific version of the lifestyle-creep problem that Chapter 7 addresses more generally.

A note on which percentage to apply where: these numbers should be tested the same way Chapter 2 recommended testing a pay-yourself-first rate — against a bad month, not a good one. If a 25% tax set-aside plus a self-paid salary still leaves the system solvent during your worst realistic income month, it's sustainable. If it doesn't, the self-paid salary is set too high relative to your income floor, not the automation itself that's broken.

Worked example

A freelancer whose monthly income has ranged from $2,400 to $9,000 over the past year sets up an income-smoothing account as the landing point for every client payment. On arrival, each deposit automatically splits: 28% to a dedicated tax account, 12% to the buffer account until it reaches a six-month reserve (a wider buffer than a salaried worker might need, given the income volatility), and the remaining 60% into the smoothing account's spendable balance. From that spendable balance, a fixed self-paid "salary" of $3,200 a month transfers out on the first of every month to the bills and spending accounts described in Chapter 3 — set conservatively, based on income floors closer to the freelancer's worst months than their best ones.

In a $2,400 month, the tax and buffer allocations are smaller in absolute terms, but the $3,200 self-paid salary still goes out, covered by the accumulated balance from stronger prior months sitting in the smoothing account. In a $9,000 month, the same percentages apply — more goes to tax, more to buffer, more into the smoothing account's balance — but the self-paid salary transfer to checking still stays at exactly $3,200, with the surplus remaining in the smoothing account rather than getting spent simply because it arrived. Over the year, the freelancer's checking account behaves exactly like a salaried employee's: a stable $3,200 landing every month, regardless of how the underlying income actually moved — because the smoothing account did the work of converting volatility into consistency before the rest of the system ever saw it.

Handling multiple income streams and irregular invoicing

Most people with variable income aren't drawing from a single client or a single source — they're often juggling several clients, projects, or platforms, each paying on its own schedule, with its own typical delay between finishing work and actually receiving payment. This adds a layer of unpredictability on top of the amount variability already covered above: not just "how much," but "when." The good news is that the two-layer system doesn't actually care how many separate deposits feed into it, or how irregular their timing is, because every deposit's first stop is the same single smoothing account regardless of source. Ten small client payments landing on ten different days behave, from the system's perspective, exactly the same as one large payment landing once — they all get the same percentage split applied on arrival, and they all ultimately fund the same fixed, predictable self-paid salary.

The practical implication is that you don't need to track income by client or by project to make this system work — you need a habit of routing every incoming payment, regardless of source, into the smoothing account first, rather than letting some payments land directly in a personal checking account out of convenience. A dedicated business or freelance-specific account, kept entirely separate from personal checking, is the cleanest way to enforce this: if every invoice is set up to pay into an account that has no other purpose, there's no ambiguity about where a given deposit is supposed to go, and no temptation to let a payment that landed somewhere convenient just stay there instead of flowing through the smoothing structure.

Quarterly estimated taxes as their own automated event

The 28% tax set-aside in the worked example above solves the "will the money exist" problem, but the "will it actually get paid to the right place, on the right schedule" problem is separate, and worth automating on its own terms. Many tax authorities require self-employed and freelance income to be paid quarterly rather than annually, and missing those quarterly deadlines can carry its own penalties independent of the total amount eventually owed. Set a recurring calendar trigger tied to each quarterly due date — well ahead of the deadline, not on it — to review the accumulated balance in the dedicated tax account and submit the payment. This isn't a step that can be fully automated end-to-end in most cases, since it typically requires an actual filing action, but the *reminder* to do it should be just as automatic as every other trigger in this book, rather than something that depends on remembering an unfamiliar, infrequent deadline correctly on your own.

A second worked example: commission-based income

A salesperson earning a modest base salary plus commission that varies significantly month to month applies the same two-layer structure with one adjustment: the base salary, being predictable, flows directly into the bills and spending accounts the way a standard paycheck would, following the mechanics from Chapters 2 and 3 without modification. Only the commission portion — the genuinely variable piece — routes through a smoothing account first. On arrival, commission payments split automatically: a portion to taxes (commission income often isn't withheld at the same rate as base salary, so the same set-aside discipline from the freelancer example applies), a portion to the buffer until it's fully funded, and the remainder either topping up a modest, fixed monthly "commission salary" transfer or, once that transfer target is reliably met, flowing directly into investing.

This hybrid approach — predictable base income automated one way, variable commission income automated another — illustrates a broader point worth carrying into the rest of this book: the mechanics in this chapter don't require an all-or-nothing choice between "salaried system" and "variable-income system." They can be applied selectively, stream by stream, to match how income actually arrives, as long as each stream's automation is internally consistent and tested against its own worst realistic case rather than borrowed uncritically from a different income pattern.

Seasonal businesses and long, predictable gaps

Some variable-income situations aren't randomly unpredictable so much as seasonally predictable — a landscaping business with almost no income over the winter months, a business tied to a specific tourist season, a role with a known slow period every year at roughly the same time. This is actually an easier case to automate for than genuinely random variability, precisely because the pattern is known in advance rather than having to be inferred after the fact. The self-paid salary from the two-layer system can be set not just against the single worst month across a full year, but calibrated specifically to survive the known slow season's full duration, with the smoothing account explicitly built up during the strong season to cover a known number of lean months ahead — closer to deliberate provisioning for a known event than a general buffer against an unknown one. Treating the slow season as a scheduled, foreseeable event (which it is) rather than an emergency (which it isn't) changes how much the buffer needs to hold and how confidently the self-paid salary can be set.

When clients or platforms pay late

A separate variability problem from income *amount* is income *timing* — invoices that go out on schedule but get paid weeks or months later than expected, which can strain even a well-designed smoothing account if the gap between expected and actual payment grows large enough. Two practical levers help here, both upstream of the automation itself: shortening payment terms on new invoices where you have the negotiating position to do so, and building the smoothing account's target balance around your typical *payment* delay, not just your income variability — if clients reliably pay 30 to 45 days after invoicing, the smoothing account needs to hold roughly that much runway on top of whatever buffer it's already carrying for amount variability, or the two-layer system will periodically run short waiting on money that's coming, just not yet.

Transitioning from employee income to variable income

A specific and common transition point is worth addressing directly: someone leaving a salaried role to start freelancing or a business, moving from a system already built around Chapters 2 and 3's predictable-paycheck mechanics into this chapter's variable-income structure. The mistake to avoid is treating this as a small tweak to the existing system rather than what it actually is — a full replacement of the income side of the architecture, even though the spending side (bills, spending, buffer, and investment accounts from Chapter 3) can largely stay as-is. The smoothing account and self-paid salary need to be built and funded *before* the transition, not after, ideally with enough of a starting reserve in the smoothing account to cover the self-paid salary through at least the first few months, since a brand-new variable-income stream typically has no track record yet to calibrate a worst-realistic-month figure against. Where possible, building that initial reserve while still receiving steady employee income — treating it as a specific, named savings goal in its own account per Chapter 3's naming convention — turns a risky income transition into a planned one.

A third worked example: a new business's first year

Someone leaving salaried work to start a small consulting practice spends the final six months of employment automatically routing extra savings into a dedicated "business transition" account, on top of their existing pay-yourself-first transfers, building roughly four months of their anticipated self-paid salary before the transition happens. Once self-employed, all client payments route into a smoothing account exactly as this chapter describes, with a self-paid salary initially set conservatively low — intentionally below what they expect the business to eventually sustain — since there's no real income history yet to test a higher figure against. Over the first year, as actual client income data accumulates, they revisit the self-paid salary figure at each quarterly review (rather than waiting a full year), gradually raising it as a genuine, evidence-based income floor becomes clear, rather than guessing at a floor on day one and hoping it holds. The pre-built four-month reserve absorbs the inevitable early unevenness while that evidence accumulates, functioning exactly as intended: a bridge between "no data yet" and "enough data to trust a real number."

Retirement contributions without an employer plan

Variable-income earners without access to an employer-sponsored retirement plan still benefit fully from Chapter 4's automation logic — the mechanic doesn't require an employer at all, only a retirement account and a recurring contribution. What changes for variable income is simply which layer the contribution attaches to: rather than a payroll deduction, the retirement contribution becomes one more automatic percentage split off the smoothing account in this chapter's two-layer structure, alongside taxes and buffer, funded the same way regardless of whether a given month was strong or lean. Because there's no employer match to anchor the funding-priority order from Chapter 4, the practical ordering for a variable-income earner without one typically becomes: taxes first (non-negotiable and immediate), buffer next until fully funded, then retirement and other investing splitting whatever percentage remains — with the specific split tested, as always, against the worst realistic month rather than an average or strong one.

The discipline of never spending directly from the smoothing account

A specific rule worth stating explicitly, because it's easy to erode without noticing: nothing gets spent directly from the smoothing account. Every dollar that leaves it does so through one of the defined channels — the tax set-aside, the buffer contribution, or the self-paid salary transfer to the bills and spending accounts from Chapter 3 — never as a direct purchase made straight from the account client payments land in. The moment a single purchase gets made directly from the smoothing account, even a reasonable and justified one, the account stops functioning as a clean conversion point between variable income and a stable salary, and starts functioning as an extra, less-disciplined spending account with an inconsistent balance. If a genuine need for extra money arises, the correct channel is a deliberate, one-time adjustment to that month's self-paid salary, decided consciously and for a clear reason — not a silent direct withdrawal that quietly breaks the boundary this chapter's entire structure depends on.

Why variable income deserves a wider buffer than salaried income

It's worth stating explicitly why this chapter's worked examples consistently size the buffer wider than the three-to-six-month range that's typical for salaried employment — six months or more, rather than three. A salaried employee's income risk is concentrated in a single, discrete event: a layoff, which is relatively rare and usually comes with some warning or severance. A variable-income earner's risk is distributed across every single month, in the form of ordinary, non-catastrophic income fluctuation that doesn't require any external trigger at all — a slow month is just a slow month, not a crisis, and it can happen with no warning and no clear external cause. Because the buffer in the two-layer system is doing double duty — both the genuine-emergency function it serves for anyone, and the income-smoothing function that's specific to variable income — it needs to be sized generously enough to absorb ordinary, expected variability without ever touching the portion reserved for genuine emergencies. Treating variable-income buffer sizing as simply "the same as salaried, just to be safe" tends to undersize it for the actual demands the two-layer system places on it.

Recognizing when variable income has become effectively stable

Some variable-income situations gradually become far more predictable over time — a freelancer with a small number of long-term retainer clients, a business with an established, repeat customer base — even though the income technically still arrives as invoiced payments rather than a fixed payroll deposit. It's worth periodically reassessing whether the full two-layer structure this chapter describes is still the right level of complexity, or whether income has become stable enough that a simpler, more direct pay-yourself-first structure from Chapter 2 would serve just as well with less overhead. There's no penalty for keeping the more conservative two-layer structure running even once income has stabilized — it costs nothing extra beyond the mild administrative overhead of an additional account — but recognizing genuine stability when it arrives, and simplifying accordingly if you choose to, keeps the system matched to reality rather than carrying more machinery than the current situation actually requires. The test is the same one this book applies everywhere else: has the worst realistic month, tracked honestly over a meaningful stretch of time, become narrow and predictable enough that the smoothing account's job is mostly already done by the underlying income itself?

Chapter 7 — Automatic Escalation

Why a Savings Rate That Never Rises Quietly Falls Behind

A pay-yourself-first system set up correctly at 12% of a given income level is a real accomplishment — but income tends to rise over a career, through raises, promotions, and new jobs, and a savings rate that stays frozen at the dollar amount set years ago quietly becomes a shrinking percentage of a growing income. Left unaddressed, this means every raise flows entirely into lifestyle — nicer everything, incrementally — rather than any of it flowing into the system that's supposed to be compounding for the future. This chapter automates the fix: a mechanism that raises your savings rate over time without requiring you to consciously revisit and re-decide it.

This is, in a real sense, the same problem Chapter 1 opened the book with, reappearing at a different point in the system's life cycle. Chapter 1 was about a static system failing to keep up with a static life that turns out to need more nuance than a single fixed percentage provides on day one. This chapter is about an otherwise well-built system failing to keep up with a life that changes after the system was already correctly built. Both are the same underlying lesson, applied at different moments: a number that was right once doesn't stay right automatically just because nothing about the automation itself broke. Something in the world around the number has to be allowed to move it, deliberately, on a schedule, or the number simply becomes wrong by omission.

What's actually happening

Lifestyle creep isn't usually one dramatic decision — it's dozens of small upgrades that each feel entirely reasonable on their own, each roughly proportional to a raise that just landed. A raise arrives, and within a few months spending has expanded to absorb nearly all of it, not through any single indulgent purchase, but through a general upward drift: a better apartment, more takeout, a nicer car payment, upgraded versions of things that were already fine before. None of these individual choices look like a mistake. Collectively, they mean the pay-yourself-first percentage set years ago, at a lower income, is still moving the exact same dollar amount it always has — while everything else has quietly scaled up around it.

The reason this drift is hard to catch manually is the same reason everything else in this book gets automated: catching it requires noticing, on your own, at an arbitrary future date, that your savings rate as a percentage of current income has fallen — a comparison nobody runs spontaneously. The fix isn't discipline about noticing. It's a trigger that raises the rate automatically, tied to the events that make lifestyle creep possible in the first place.

It's worth being precise about what makes lifestyle creep genuinely difficult to fight with willpower alone, since it's a slightly different mechanism than the spending erosion covered in Chapter 1. Chapter 1's erosion happens because undirected money sits somewhere convenient to spend. Lifestyle creep happens even to money that was never undirected — a percentage that was deliberately, correctly set at one income level simply stops being the right percentage once income changes, through no failure of the original decision at all. The number was right when it was chosen. It just wasn't built to update itself, and nothing in a static system prompts anyone to revisit it. This is precisely why escalation deserves its own chapter rather than being treated as a minor addendum to Chapter 2 — it's solving a fundamentally different problem: not "how do I make the first decision automatic," but "how do I make sure a correct decision doesn't quietly become an incorrect one as circumstances change around it."

The framework: escalation triggers, not calendar dates

1. Tie escalation to raises, not the calendar. The single cleanest trigger: any time take-home pay increases — a raise, a promotion, a new job — a fixed portion of the increase (a common approach is roughly half) is automatically redirected into the pay-yourself-first percentage from Chapter 2, before the new, higher paycheck ever gets a chance to establish a new, higher spending baseline. The other half is genuinely available to enjoy — this isn't about capturing every dollar of every raise, which tends to feel punishing and doesn't survive contact with real motivation. It's about making sure at least some of every increase compounds instead of all of it evaporating into lifestyle.

2. Automate the redirect at the source, the same day the raise takes effect. If a raise increases take-home pay by $300 a month, the automatic transfer percentages or fixed amounts from Chapters 2 and 3 should be updated in the same sitting the new pay lands — not "at some point," which functionally means never, because there's no natural prompt to revisit it later. Treat a raise as the trigger event itself, the same way a paycheck date triggers the original pay-yourself-first transfer.

3. Use windfalls as one-time escalation events, not spending events. Tax refunds, bonuses, and other irregular lump sums are a second natural escalation trigger, separate from raises. Rather than treating a windfall purely as spending money, route a majority of it directly into the investment or buffer accounts from Chapter 3, and treat the decision as already made in advance — before the money arrives — rather than something to decide once it's sitting in the account and competing against every discretionary purchase, per Chapter 1's core mechanic.

4. Set a floor escalation on a fixed schedule, as a backstop. Even without a raise, a modest scheduled increase —

for instance, raising the pay-yourself-first percentage by half a percentage point once a year, on the same date every year — keeps the system from staying static indefinitely, and functions as a low-effort default for periods where no specific raise event triggers a manual update.

Worked example

Someone starts with the 12% pay-yourself-first rate from Chapter 2's example, on a $4,800 monthly income. Over the following two years, they receive two raises: one bringing take-home pay to $5,100, another to $5,500. Each time, the same week the new pay takes effect, they redirect half of the increase into their automated transfers. The first raise adds $300 a month; $150 of it goes into the pay-yourself-first allocations, $150 becomes available spending. The second raise adds another $400; again, $200 escalates the savings transfers, $200 becomes available spending.

By the end of the two years, their automatic pay-yourself-first transfer has grown from $576 a month to $926 a month — not through a single deliberate decision to "save more," which tends to fail exactly as fixed-willpower plans fail elsewhere in this book, but through a series of small, automatic redirections triggered by events that were already happening anyway. Meanwhile, their available spending has also grown, from $824 a month to $1,224 — real lifestyle improvement, just not 100% of the increase. The system captured roughly half of two years of raises into compounding accounts, and the other half genuinely improved day-to-day life, without a single month requiring a conscious "let's revisit our savings rate" conversation.

Escalation on variable income

Applying escalation to the variable-income system from Chapter 6 requires a small translation, since there's no single "raise" event to anchor the trigger to. The workable equivalent is a periodic review — every six or twelve months is reasonable — of the income floor the self-paid salary is built against. If a freelancer's worst realistic month has genuinely and durably improved (not just one unusually strong quarter, but a sustained shift in typical client volume or rates), that's the freelance version of a raise, and it justifies raising both the self-paid salary and the percentage split feeding buffer and investing, following the same "roughly half compounds, half goes to lifestyle" principle from the salaried version. The key discipline is not mistaking a single good month for a durable floor increase — escalating the fixed salary too early, based on one strong month rather than a genuine trend, reintroduces exactly the fragility Chapter 6 was built to eliminate.

Escalating as a household, without one person's raise silently subsidizing drift

In a household with the parallel dual-income structure from Chapter 1's second worked example, escalation works cleanest when each income's raise triggers its own proportional escalation, rather than pooling raises and making a joint decision about the combined total. If one partner receives a substantial raise and the other doesn't, escalating only the raised income's automated percentage — rather than quietly letting the whole household's spending rise to match the new combined total — keeps the mechanic honest and prevents one person's career progress from being absorbed entirely into shared lifestyle inflation without any of it compounding for the household's shared future.

Downshifting an escalation that turns out to be unsustainable

Occasionally an escalation, tested reasonably at the time, turns out in practice not to hold — a raise was smaller in take-home terms than expected after a change in tax withholding or benefits costs, for instance. When this happens, the correct response is a deliberate downshift, not silent erosion. Explicitly reduce the automated percentage back to a sustainable level, using the same bad-month test from Chapter 2, rather than letting the transfer simply start failing or bouncing on tight months, which is the outcome that actually damages trust in the system. A consciously chosen, slightly lower savings rate that holds reliably is a better outcome than an aspirational higher one that has to be manually rescued every few months — the entire premise of this book is that a rate you don't have to think about beats a rate you do, even if the number itself is smaller.

Worked example, continued: a plateau year

In the third year following the two raises above, income stays flat with no further raise. The scheduled floor escalation from this chapter's framework — the modest, fixed annual increase used as a backstop even without a specific raise event — adds a small, automatic half-percentage-point bump to the pay-yourself-first rate on its scheduled date regardless. The increase is small enough not to require a bad-month retest (it's well within the margin already validated at the prior rate), and it keeps the system from sitting perfectly static during a year that otherwise offered no natural escalation trigger. This is the entire value of having a backstop trigger in addition to event-based ones: the system keeps making small, forward progress even during years where nothing dramatic happens to prompt it.

Why capturing every dollar of a raise usually backfires

It's tempting to design an escalation rule that redirects the full amount of every raise into savings, on the logic that you were living fine on the old amount, so you don't "need" any of the increase. In practice, this version of the rule tends to fail more often than the roughly-half version described earlier in this chapter, for a reason worth naming directly: a rule that captures 100% of every raise means your day-to-day lifestyle never improves no matter how much your income grows, which removes any felt reward from career progress and makes the automated system feel punitive rather than beneficial. A rule people can feel good about is one they're far more likely to leave alone indefinitely, which is the actual goal — an aggressive rule that gets manually overridden every time a raise lands provides less long-run benefit than a moderate rule that's never touched. Roughly half is a reasonable default; the exact split matters less than choosing a split you can genuinely live with long enough for it to compound.

Milestone escalation as an alternative to percentage-based triggers

An alternative to tying escalation strictly to raises or a fixed calendar date is tying it to specific milestones reaching completion — the buffer account hitting its full target, a specific debt being paid off, a medium-term goal account reaching its target and closing out. Each of these milestones frees up money that was previously earmarked for a purpose that no longer exists, and redirecting that freed-up amount into the pay-yourself-first rate, rather than letting it default into discretionary spending simply because its prior job ended, is a natural and often larger escalation opportunity than the incremental raise-based approach alone. The two approaches aren't exclusive — a well-built system typically escalates on several of these triggers over time: raises, windfalls, the annual floor bump, and milestone completions, each contributing its own increment as the relevant event actually happens.

The compounding case for escalating early rather than late

The specific numbers in this chapter's worked examples matter less than the timing principle behind them: an escalation captured early in a saving or investing timeline has dramatically more time to compound than the identical escalation captured a decade later, even though the dollar amount redirected is the same in both cases. This is a straightforward consequence of how compounding works over time, not a claim about any specific market return, but it's worth stating plainly because it's the strongest practical argument for building the escalation habit now rather than waiting for "a bigger raise that's worth bothering with." A modest early escalation, left alone to compound for two or three decades, generally outperforms a larger escalation started a decade later — which means the specific size of the raise triggering an escalation matters far less than simply having the escalation mechanism running as early as possible.

Escalation fatigue and how to avoid it

A subtle risk with escalation, particularly the raise-triggered version, is a kind of fatigue that sets in if every single pay increase, no matter how small, triggers a formal redirect-half-of-it ritual — over years, with enough small raises, this can start to feel like a recurring chore rather than an automatic background process, which risks the exact abandonment problem Chapter 8 addresses for the system more broadly. The practical fix is to set a minimum threshold below which small raises simply flow to spending without triggering a formal escalation event — a cost-of-living adjustment of a percent or two, for instance, might reasonably be left alone, while a genuine promotion or a job change with a substantial pay jump triggers the full redirect-and-update process. This keeps the escalation mechanism reserved for the moments it actually matters, rather than turning it into a small administrative task attached to every single paycheck change, however minor.

Escalation as a career-long habit, not a one-time fix

It's worth stepping back and naming what this chapter is actually building toward across an entire working life, not just the next raise or two. A savings rate that was reasonable at twenty-five, on an entry-level income, is very likely too low by forty, after a decade or two of career growth — not because the twenty-five-year-old made a mistake, but because circumstances changed and the rate never got the chance to change with them. The alternative to automatic escalation isn't a static rate that stays perfectly fine forever; it's a rate that quietly becomes worse and worse relative to actual income and actual opportunity to save, year after year, unless something explicitly counteracts that drift. Escalation is that counteracting force, and it's worth thinking of it less as a chapter-specific tactic and more as a permanent feature that should run for the entire span of a working career — every raise, every windfall, every milestone, every year, contributing its own small increment, for decades, the same way compounding itself works quietly in the background the entire time.

Escalation and major life-stage transitions

Certain life transitions change the entire shape of what a reasonable savings rate looks like, independent of any specific raise — a first home purchase that shifts a large share of income toward a mortgage, a new dependent that adds significant new fixed costs, a return to school that temporarily reduces income while increasing future earning potential. These moments don't fit neatly into the raise-triggered or milestone-triggered escalation patterns described earlier in this chapter, because they're not really escalation events at all — they're the kind of structural life change that Chapter 8 categorizes as warranting a full system review rather than a routine escalation increment. It's worth explicitly distinguishing the two: an escalation event adds to an existing, working system without disturbing its foundations, while a life-stage transition often requires rebuilding the foundations themselves — new fixed-cost figures, a retested pay-yourself-first percentage, potentially a different buffer target. Treating a life-stage transition as if it were just another escalation trigger, and bolting a small increment onto an otherwise unchanged system, risks leaving the system calibrated against a version of your life that no longer exists.

Escalation isn't only about the percentage

Everything in this chapter has focused on raising the pay-yourself-first percentage over time, but it's worth noting that escalation, as a general principle, applies to more than just that single number. The buffer target itself deserves periodic escalation as fixed costs rise — three months of expenses at an earlier, lower cost-of-living figure is no longer three months of expenses once rent or other fixed costs have grown, even if the buffer's dollar balance hasn't changed. The investment contribution's dollar figure, if it was set as a fixed amount rather than a percentage per the discussion in Chapter 2, needs the same periodic reconsideration. Even the flex fund's sizing, covered in Chapter 8, benefits from the same escalation logic as life circumstances change the pattern of irregular spending. Treat escalation less as a single mechanic applied to one number, and more as a standing principle applied to every number in this book: every fixed figure was calibrated against a specific moment in your financial life, and every one of them deserves periodic reconsideration as that moment recedes further into the past.

Tracking escalation's cumulative effect over time

Because each individual escalation increment tends to be modest — half of a raise, a small annual bump, a redirected debt payment — it's easy to lose sight of how much the pay-yourself-first rate has actually grown over several years of consistent escalation, since no single increase feels dramatic in isolation. It's worth keeping a simple running record, even just a note with a date and a percentage, each time the rate changes, so you can look back after several years and see the full cumulative shift at once, rather than only ever perceiving it one small increment at a time. Seeing a savings rate that's grown from 10% to 18% over five years, laid out plainly, tends to reinforce the value of the whole escalation habit far more effectively than any single increment did on its own — a useful piece of positive feedback that helps the habit stay in place for the following five years as well.

Chapter 8 — Building In Flexibility Without Breaking the System

Why a System With No Give Eventually Gets Abandoned Entirely

Every mechanic in this book so far is built around removing decisions and making the correct behavior automatic. Taken too far, that same rigidity becomes a liability: a system with zero flexibility for a genuinely unusual month — a wedding, a big trip, an unexpected large expense that isn't quite an emergency — tends to get disabled entirely rather than adjusted, because there's no sanctioned way to bend it without turning it off. This chapter is about building deliberate, bounded flexibility into the system, so it survives real life instead of getting abandoned the first time real life doesn't cooperate with it.

If the first seven chapters of this book have felt, at points, like an argument for maximal rigidity — every decision automated, every dollar assigned a job, every percentage locked against a bad-month test — this chapter is where that argument gets its necessary counterweight. A system too rigid to bend at all doesn't actually outperform a flexible one over a long enough timeline; it just fails differently, and often more abruptly, when it finally does fail. The chapters that came before this one built the discipline. This one builds the shock absorbers. Both are required for the same reason a well-engineered structure needs both a strong frame and some built-in give: strength without flexibility doesn't survive contact with the unpredictable forces a real life, lived over decades, is guaranteed to apply to it eventually.

What's actually happening

An all-or-nothing automated system creates a particular failure mode: the first month it genuinely doesn't fit — income was tighter than usual, or a real one-time expense came up — there's no middle path between "let the automation run and overdraft the checking account" and "pause all the automation." Faced with that choice, most people pause everything, and "temporarily paused" quietly becomes permanent, because restarting a paused system requires exactly the kind of active decision this whole book is designed to avoid needing.

The fix isn't to loosen the system generally — that reintroduces the erosion problem from Chapter 1. It's to build specific, pre-planned exceptions into the system in advance, so that when a genuinely unusual month arrives, there's a sanctioned adjustment already available rather than a binary choice between running the system broken or shutting it off.

This is worth framing as a design principle that generalizes well beyond personal finance: any system meant to run unattended for years needs a defined tolerance for deviation built in from the start, or the first deviation it encounters becomes an existential threat to the whole system rather than a routine, absorbable event. A bridge engineered with zero tolerance for thermal expansion cracks the first hot summer. A financial system engineered with zero tolerance for an unusual month breaks the first time one arrives. The fix in both cases is the same: build the tolerance in deliberately, at the design stage, rather than discovering the need for it under pressure, in the moment the system is already being tested by circumstances nobody planned for.

The framework: bounded flexibility, decided in advance

1. Build a "flex fund" as its own account, funded automatically like everything else. A modest automatic transfer — even $50 to $100 a month — into a dedicated account explicitly earmarked for planned irregular expenses: gifts, travel, seasonal costs, home maintenance. Because it's funded automatically and has its own account, spending from it doesn't touch the buffer, the investments, or the bills accounts, and doesn't require disabling anything else. This single change eliminates most of the situations that would otherwise tempt someone to pause their entire automated system.

2. Pre-decide the rules for adjusting the pay-yourself-first rate, before you need to use them. Rather than deciding in the moment, under pressure, whether to lower a savings transfer during a tight month, decide the rule in advance: for instance, the rate can be temporarily reduced (never eliminated entirely) for up to two consecutive months, with an automatic reminder to review and restore it on the third month. A pre-agreed rule, decided with a clear head, is a very different thing from an emergency decision made mid-crisis — and it's far more likely to actually get followed and reversed, rather than becoming a permanent quiet reduction nobody revisits.

3. Distinguish a real emergency from a preference for more spending money. The buffer account exists specifically for the former. A useful test before pulling from it: would this expense, left unaddressed, create a worse financial or practical outcome than spending the money would prevent? A broken car that's your only way to work clears that bar. A vacation that would be nice but isn't urgent doesn't — that's what the flex fund from point one is for. Keeping this distinction explicit, rather than deciding case-by-case under emotional pressure, prevents the buffer account from being slowly drained by expenses that were never really emergencies.

4. Review, don't rebuild, when life changes structurally. A new job, a move, a new dependent, a significant change in fixed costs — these are legitimate reasons to revisit percentages and amounts across the entire system, not just make an ad hoc exception. The distinction matters: an exception is a temporary, pre-bounded deviation from a system that stays otherwise intact;

a review is a deliberate, whole-system recalibration in response to a genuine structural change. Treating every deviation as a full rebuild is exhausting and tends to result in the system just not getting rebuilt. Treating every structural change as a minor exception means the system slowly drifts out of sync with actual life. Both failure modes are avoided by keeping the two processes clearly separate.

Worked example

Someone running the full system from Chapters 1 through 7 hits a month where an out-of-town family event adds $600 in travel costs they hadn't planned for. Because they've been automatically funding a $75-a-month flex account for the past year, $900 is sitting there specifically for cases like this — the expense is covered without touching the buffer, without reducing the investment transfer, and without a single other part of the system needing to change. No decision was required in the moment beyond "yes, this qualifies," because the account and its purpose were both decided long before the trip came up.

Three months later, a slower stretch of client work drops their income below their usual floor for two consecutive months. Per their pre-agreed rule, they temporarily reduce (not eliminate) their pay-yourself-first transfer by a third for those two months, with a calendar reminder already set to review and restore it on month three. When month three arrives, income has recovered, and the reminder prompts them to restore the full rate — a five-minute check-in, rather than a system that quietly stayed reduced because nobody remembered to revisit it. In both cases, the system bent exactly as far as it was designed to bend, and then returned to its default shape — which is the entire difference between flexibility and collapse.

Sizing the flex fund correctly

A flex fund that's too small doesn't cover the situations it's meant to cover, and defeats its own purpose by forcing exactly the buffer-raid or system-pause decision it exists to prevent. A flex fund that's too large starts quietly functioning as a second, less-disciplined spending account, undermining the honest-balance principle from Chapter 3. A reasonable way to size it: look back over the last twelve to eighteen months and total up the genuinely irregular, non-emergency expenses that came up — gifts, a friend's wedding, a annual family trip, a home repair that wasn't quite an emergency but wasn't optional either. Divide that annual total by twelve, and that's a defensible starting point for the monthly flex transfer. It won't be perfectly accurate in the first year, but it's a real number grounded in your own actual pattern of irregular spending, rather than an arbitrary guess — and it can be adjusted at the next quarterly review once you have a clearer read on whether it ran short or built up an unused surplus.

A cooling-off period for anything that doesn't clearly fit

Some expenses won't cleanly sort into "buffer-worthy emergency," "flex-fund-worthy planned irregularity," or "this month's discretionary spending" — a genuinely tempting large purchase that isn't urgent but also isn't trivial. For anything in that ambiguous middle, a simple, pre-decided rule works better than a case-by-case judgment call made in the moment of temptation: a mandatory 48- or 72-hour waiting period between deciding you want to make the purchase and actually making it, during which no account gets touched at all. This isn't about denying the purchase — it's about separating the decision from the initial emotional pull that prompted it. Purchases that still feel worth making after the waiting period usually are. A large number of them don't survive the wait, which is itself useful information about how much the purchase was actually wanted versus how much it was an in-the-moment impulse.

A second worked example: the holiday season

Holiday spending is one of the most predictable sources of flex-fund pressure, and one of the easiest to plan for precisely because it recurs on the same known schedule every year. Rather than treating each December as a surprise that requires pulling from the buffer or pausing other transfers, someone running the full system reviews the prior year's actual holiday spending during their fall quarterly review and finds it ran close to $800 across gifts, travel, and hosting. They adjust their flex-fund transfer upward slightly from September through November specifically, front-loading the fund ahead of the season it's meant to cover, then let the transfer drop back to its normal level in December once the fund has already accumulated what's needed.

This is a useful pattern beyond the holiday example specifically: recurring irregular expenses that show up on a *predictable* calendar — an annual insurance renewal, a yearly subscription bundle, a seasonal cost — don't actually need to be treated as irregular at all, once you've tracked them for a year or two. They can be scheduled, front-loaded, and absorbed into the flex fund's timing deliberately, rather than treated as a recurring surprise that has to be reacted to fresh each time it arrives.

The difference between flexibility and inconsistency

It's worth drawing a sharp line between the deliberate, bounded flexibility this chapter builds and the kind of inconsistency this entire book exists to eliminate. Flexibility is pre-planned: a flex fund with a defined purpose and size, a pre-agreed rule for temporarily reducing the pay-yourself-first rate with a built-in review date, a defined test for what qualifies as a real emergency. Inconsistency is undefined: pausing a transfer "just this once" with no plan to restart it, dipping into the buffer for something that doesn't clearly meet the emergency test because it's convenient in the moment, adjusting a percentage on a whim during a stressful week with no review date attached. The external behavior in the moment can look identical — money moved, a transfer skipped — but the difference is entirely about whether the deviation was decided in advance, with a clear head, and bounded by a defined return-to-normal condition. A system that allows for the first kind of flexibility survives real life. A system that allows for the second kind eventually stops functioning as a system at all and becomes, in practice, the exact ad hoc approach this book was written to replace.

A brief note on shared flexibility in a household

Where a household runs the dual-income structure described earlier in this book, the flex fund and the temporary-reduction rule work best when both partners have visibility into them and have agreed to the same bounded rules in advance, rather than each person independently deciding, in their own head, what counts as an acceptable exception. A shared, explicit rule — documented somewhere both people can reference, even something as simple as a shared note — prevents the situation where one partner treats a given expense as obviously flex-fund-worthy and the other treats the same expense as an overreach, a disagreement that's far easier to have once, calmly, while setting the rule, than repeatedly, in the moment, each time a borderline expense comes up.

How much flexibility is actually healthy

There's a version of this chapter's advice that could be misread as license to bend the system constantly, provided each bend is technically pre-planned. That's not the intent, and it's worth being explicit about the difference between a system that flexes occasionally, as designed, and one that's flexing so often the "exception" has effectively become the norm. A useful check: if the flex fund is being drawn down every single month rather than occasionally, or if the temporary-reduction rule from this chapter gets invoked more months than not, that's not evidence the flexibility mechanism is working — it's evidence the underlying percentages and amounts from Chapters 2 and 3 were never actually calibrated to reality in the first place, and belong back at the bad-month test rather than papered over with an increasingly routine exception. Flexibility is meant to absorb genuinely unusual months. If most months qualify as unusual, the baseline itself, not the flexibility layer sitting on top of it, is what needs to change.

Revisiting flex-fund sizing over time

The sizing formula described earlier in this chapter — averaging the last twelve to eighteen months of genuinely irregular expenses — should itself be revisited periodically rather than set once and left alone indefinitely, since life stages change the shape of irregular spending considerably. A flex fund sized for a single person's occasional gifts and travel will likely undersize once a wedding, a growing family, or a change in social obligations shifts the pattern of irregular costs meaningfully. Treat the flex-fund amount the same way this book treats every other number in the system: tested against real data, revisited on a fixed schedule, and adjusted deliberately rather than left to quietly become wrong.

Flexibility as the thing that makes the rest of the book trustworthy

It's worth being direct about why this chapter exists roughly two-thirds of the way through the book, after seven chapters of building progressively stricter automation, rather than being treated as an afterthought. A system with no sanctioned flexibility is a system people will eventually break on purpose, out of simple necessity, the first time real life doesn't fit its assumptions — and once it's been broken once without a clean way to repair it, trust in the whole structure erodes, making every subsequent override feel more justified than the last. This chapter is what keeps that erosion from starting in the first place. By building the flex fund, the bounded temporary-reduction rule, and the clear emergency test in advance, the system earns the kind of trust that lets it keep running for years rather than months — not because it never bends, but because every bend has a defined shape and a defined return to normal, which is the entire difference between a system that survives contact with an actual life and one that only ever worked in the planning document.

Special occasions that deserve their own planning, not just flex-fund coverage

Some irregular expenses are large and predictable enough — a wedding, a milestone anniversary trip, a significant home renovation — that routing them through the general flex fund described earlier in this chapter would either overwhelm it or require setting the flex fund's ongoing size unrealistically high to accommodate a single, unusual event. These deserve the same treatment Chapter 3 gives any other major, named goal: a dedicated account, funded by its own automatic transfer, sized against a real target and a real timeline, kept entirely separate from the general-purpose flex fund. Treating a wedding as "just a bigger version of holiday spending" and routing it through the same account that covers routine irregular costs blurs two very different kinds of planning together — one recurring and modest, the other large and one-time — and tends to leave both underfunded. When a major, named, one-time event is on the horizon, give it the dignity of its own account and its own automatic contribution, calculated backward from the target amount and the target date the same way any goal account in this book is built.

A pre-decided list of what does and doesn't qualify as an emergency

Because the emergency test from earlier in this chapter — "would this, left unaddressed, create a worse outcome than spending the money would prevent" — still leaves some room for interpretation in the moment, it helps to pre-populate a short, concrete list of examples during a calm period, rather than relying purely on the abstract test under pressure. A reasonable starting list of genuine buffer-account qualifiers: a job loss or major reduction in income, an urgent medical or dental cost not otherwise covered, a necessary repair to a primary vehicle that's your only way to work, an unavoidable home repair that threatens habitability (a failed furnace in winter, a serious leak). A reasonable list of things that don't qualify, however tempting in the moment: a limited-time sale on something you'd wanted anyway, a spontaneous trip invitation, an upgrade to something that's still functioning fine, a purchase driven mainly by comparison to what someone else has. Having this list written down in the same document as the rest of your system's rules turns a fraught, emotionally loaded judgment call into a quick lookup against a standard you set for yourself with a clear head.

Flexibility that expires

Every exception this chapter sanctions should carry an expiration built in from the moment it's invoked, not just a general intention to revisit it eventually. A temporarily reduced pay-yourself-first rate without a specific restoration date attached tends to simply become the new permanent rate, quietly, without anyone ever deciding that outright — nobody consciously chooses to abandon the higher rate, it just never gets restored because there was no specific date forcing the question back onto the calendar. Every time this chapter's flexibility mechanisms get used — a temporary reduction, a buffer withdrawal, a flex-fund draw — attach a specific date or a specific triggering condition for reviewing and, where appropriate, reversing it. An exception without an expiration date isn't really an exception. It's a silent, permanent change to the system that happened to arrive wearing the label of a temporary one.

Logging exceptions instead of just remembering them

A short, ongoing log of every time this chapter's flexibility mechanisms actually get invoked — a single line noting the date, what was drawn on, how much, and the review date attached to it — turns an abstract intention to "track exceptions" into a concrete habit that survives busy weeks and imperfect memory. This log serves two purposes beyond the immediate tracking: it gives the quarterly review from Chapter 9 something concrete to check off (has every logged exception actually been reviewed and, where appropriate, reversed by its stated date), and it gives you, over a year or two, real data about how often the system is actually flexing and in which direction — informing exactly the "how much flexibility is healthy" assessment covered earlier in this chapter. A system's flexibility mechanisms, like every other automated piece of this book, work best when they leave a trail rather than depending entirely on memory to enforce their own boundaries.

Chapter 9 — Common Tactical Mistakes

Why Systems That Look Correct on Paper Still Fail in Practice

Most automated money systems don't fail because the underlying logic was wrong — they fail because of small implementation mistakes that undermine the logic without anyone noticing until months or years later. This chapter catalogs the mistakes that show up most often, so you can check your own system against them directly rather than discovering them the hard way.

There's a common thread worth naming before working through the individual mistakes: nearly all of them are quiet rather than dramatic. None of the ten below announce themselves with an obvious crisis the way, say, a job loss does. A percentage tested against the wrong month doesn't fail loudly on day one — it holds up fine for months, sometimes years, until the first genuinely tight stretch reveals the gap. Cash sitting uninvested in a brokerage account doesn't trigger an alert — it just quietly fails to compound, invisibly, for however long it goes unnoticed. This is precisely why they belong in their own chapter, separate from the specific mechanics chapters that introduced each one: a mistake that doesn't announce itself needs a deliberate, periodic check to catch, rather than a wait for it to become obvious on its own.

Read this chapter as a diagnostic checklist rather than a list to memorize in order. If your own system is already running, the more useful way to use what follows is to hold each mistake up against your actual accounts and transfers, one at a time, and ask honestly whether it applies. A handful of these will almost certainly apply to any real system that's been running for more than a year or two without a structured review — that's not a sign the system was poorly built, it's simply what happens to any unattended structure over time, which is exactly why Chapter 9 exists as a standing, recurring practice rather than a one-time setup task.

Mistake one: automating a percentage that was never tested against a bad month

Covered in Chapter 2, but worth restating because it's the single most common root cause of abandoned systems: a pay-yourself-first rate set against an average or good month, rather than a realistic bad one, works fine until the first genuinely tight month arrives — at which point the automatic transfer either overdrafts the account or forces an emergency manual override. One overdraft is often enough to make someone distrust the entire system and quietly turn it off. Test every percentage against the worst realistic case before automating it, not the best or average case.

Mistake two: leaving cash uninvested "temporarily" inside a brokerage account

Covered in Chapter 4: automating the transfer into a brokerage account without also automating the purchase inside it leaves cash sitting there, waiting for a decision that keeps getting deferred. Money that's technically "in the investment account" but not actually invested isn't doing the job it was moved there to do. If a recurring automatic purchase isn't available for your specific investment choice, set a recurring calendar reminder tightly coupled to the transfer date, so the gap between transfer and purchase is measured in a day or two, not months.

Mistake three: treating the buffer account like a second checking account

An emergency fund with a debit card attached to it, or one that's too easy to transfer from with a single tap, stops functioning as a buffer and starts functioning as overflow spending money. The entire value of a separate buffer account is the friction between it and your spending — remove the friction, and you've effectively merged it back into checking, just with an optimistic label. Keep it at a separate institution, without a linked card, with at least a one-to-three-day transfer delay if the platform allows it.

Mistake four: setting up the system once and never re-testing it against reality

A system built correctly for a $4,500 monthly income and a specific set of fixed costs will quietly drift out of alignment as both change — rent goes up, income changes, a new recurring cost appears. Because the system runs without requiring attention, it's easy to assume it's still correct indefinitely. A brief quarterly check — not a full rebuild, just a comparison of what's actually happening in each account against what the system was designed to do — catches this drift before it becomes a real gap. Pair this check with the subscription audit from Chapter 5; they're natural to run on the same recurring calendar trigger.

Mistake five: automating investment contributions without automating an asset allocation decision

Setting up a recurring transfer and purchase, per Chapter 4, only works cleanly if there's already a decided, appropriate allocation for the money to buy into. Automating a contribution into a single stock, or into whatever fund happened to be the default when the account was opened, without a deliberate allocation decision behind it, converts a genuinely good mechanic (consistent contribution) into a genuinely risky one (consistent concentration in something that was never actually chosen). The automation should sit on top of a real allocation decision, not substitute for one.

Mistake six: building the entire system around a single institution with no redundancy

Keeping every account — bills, spending, buffer, investing — at the same bank or platform means a single account freeze, fraud flag, or technical outage can lock up the entire system at once, including the buffer account that's specifically meant to be available during a crisis. Spreading the accounts across at least two separate institutions means a problem at one doesn't take down the whole structure simultaneously.

Mistake seven: confusing "automated" with "unmonitored"

The entire point of this book is removing the need for constant manual decisions — not removing all oversight permanently. A system that's never reviewed, even quarterly, will eventually contain an error nobody catches: a transfer that silently failed, a subscription audit that never got redone, a percentage that made sense two incomes ago. Automation should reduce the frequency of attention required, from constant to occasional — not eliminate it entirely. Chapter 8's quarterly review habit exists precisely to prevent this mistake.

Mistake eight: ignoring account fees that quietly erode the system's own output

An account with a monthly maintenance fee, a below-market interest rate on a buffer account, or a brokerage with high expense ratios on its default fund options doesn't announce itself as a problem — it just means a portion of every automated contribution is being silently offset before it ever gets the chance to compound. Because these costs are automatic themselves, they suffer from the exact same invisibility problem as the forgotten subscriptions in Chapter 5, just on the savings side of the ledger instead of the spending side. Worth including account fees and yields explicitly in the same quarterly review that catches subscription creep — comparing your buffer account's actual interest rate and your investment account's fee structure against what's genuinely available elsewhere periodically, rather than assuming the accounts you set up years ago are still competitive today.

Mistake nine: vague account names that lead to misdirected transfers

A system with five or six accounts, several of them generically labeled "Savings" or "Savings 2" across two different banks, creates a real risk of setting up a transfer to the wrong destination — sending an investment contribution into what was meant to be the buffer, for instance, purely because two accounts looked similar enough in a dropdown menu during setup. This isn't a hypothetical edge case; it's a routine, easy-to-make error precisely because the entire point of this book's account architecture is to reduce how much attention you pay to each individual transfer once it's set up — which means a mislabeling mistake made once at setup can persist, unnoticed, for a long time. The fix from Chapter 3 — naming every account explicitly by its job — isn't just about psychological friction at the point of spending; it's also a direct defense against this specific setup error, since a clearly labeled destination is much harder to select incorrectly than a generic one.

Mistake ten: automating aggressive investing before addressing high-interest debt

Automation makes it easy to set up an investment contribution and forget about it — which is exactly the goal for money that should be invested, but a mistake when the money in question could instead be paying down debt carrying a cost higher than any reasonable expected investment return. Automating an investment contribution before that kind of debt is addressed isn't wrong in every case, particularly where an employer match makes the first slice of investing close to a guaranteed return (Chapter 4 covers this ordering explicitly) — but investing aggressively beyond that match while high-interest debt sits untouched, purely because the investment contribution is easier to automate and feels more rewarding than a debt payment, is a common and costly sequencing error. Revisit Chapter 4's funding order before scaling any investment automation up: employer match first, then genuinely high-cost debt, then the rest of tax-advantaged and taxable investing.

Why these mistakes cluster together

Look back across all ten, and a pattern emerges: nearly every one of them is a version of the same underlying failure — a piece of the system was set up once, under one set of assumptions, and never revisited as those assumptions changed. A percentage tested against a good month instead of a bad one. Cash left uninvested because the second automation step was never built. A buffer account that quietly gained a debit card at some point. Fixed costs that grew without the automated transfers growing to match. None of these are failures of the automation itself — the transfers keep firing exactly as configured, which is precisely the problem, because "exactly as configured" stops being correct the moment life underneath the configuration changes and nobody updates it.

This is the entire argument for the quarterly review habit that's threaded through every chapter of this book, restated here directly: automation removes the need for *constant* attention, not *all* attention, ever, forever. A system checked four times a year for drift, misconfiguration, and outdated assumptions catches essentially every mistake on this list before it compounds into a real problem. A system set up once and never looked at again will, eventually, contain most of them.

A short checklist for the quarterly review itself

Since several chapters in this book point back to the same recurring quarterly review without ever fully consolidating what belongs in it, it's worth gathering the full list here in one place. A complete quarterly review, in practice, touches: the recurring-cost inventory from Chapter 5 (cancel, downgrade, negotiate); the pay-yourself-first percentage from Chapter 2, retested against the most recent genuinely tight month rather than assumed still valid; the account balances across the four structural accounts from Chapter 3, checked for drift into unintended purposes; the investment contribution from Chapter 4, confirmed as still actually being invested rather than sitting as uninvested cash; the flex-fund balance and sizing from Chapter 8, compared against actual usage over the quarter; and, for anyone on the variable-income system from Chapter 6, the self-paid salary figure, checked against the most recent data on the true income floor.

Not every one of these needs deep attention every single quarter — some quarters will turn up nothing to change, and that's a fine outcome, not a wasted review. The point of the checklist isn't to guarantee something gets fixed every time; it's to guarantee something gets *looked at* every time, on a schedule, rather than depending on a problem becoming visible enough to force attention on its own. By the time a misconfigured system becomes visible without a deliberate check, it's usually already cost real money for months.

Mistakes that look like automation problems but aren't

Occasionally what looks like a flaw in the automated system is actually a flaw somewhere else entirely — a change in tax withholding that makes a paycheck smaller than expected, a billing error from a service provider, a one-time irregular expense that happened to land the same week as a scheduled transfer and created the appearance of the system failing. Before concluding that a percentage or account structure needs to change, it's worth confirming the actual root cause first, since adjusting a well-calibrated system in response to a one-time external event, rather than a genuine structural mismatch, reintroduces unnecessary instability into something that was working correctly. The bad-month test throughout this book is specifically about *recurring* worst-case conditions, not one-off anomalies — a system doesn't need to be rebuilt around a single unusual week, only around a pattern that's likely to recur.

Building resistance to well-meaning bad advice

Once a working automated system is in place, it will periodically be challenged by well-intentioned advice from people who aren't operating under the same constraints — a suggestion to chase a trendy investment because a friend did well with it, a comment that automating your savings is "too rigid" or "not spontaneous enough," pressure to redirect money from the buffer or investment accounts toward a discretionary purchase because "you deserve it" after a hard stretch. None of this advice is necessarily malicious, and some of it may even be well-suited to the person giving it, given their own circumstances. But a system that gets renegotiated every time someone offers a compelling-sounding reason to deviate from it stops being a system and becomes, again, a series of individual decisions made under social or emotional pressure — precisely the failure mode this entire book is built to prevent. The practical defense isn't to become closed off to genuinely useful input, but to hold a clear standard for what actually justifies changing the system: a documented bad-month test that no longer holds, a genuine structural life change, or a mistake caught during a scheduled review — not a single compelling conversation, however persuasive, that didn't go through that same process.

The mistake of comparing your system to someone else's numbers

A related trap deserves its own callout: hearing a specific number from someone else — a coworker's savings rate, a friend's investment account balance, a stranger's account of an unusually good year — and using it to judge your own system's percentages, rather than continuing to test your own numbers against your own worst realistic month and your own goals. Every number in this book is meant to be derived from your specific fixed costs, income pattern, and risk tolerance, not imported wholesale from someone else's circumstances, which are very unlikely to genuinely match yours in the ways that matter for the bad-month test. A savings rate that's objectively lower than someone else's, but that survives every real month of your actual life without needing rescue, is doing its job better than a borrowed, higher number that gets quietly abandoned within a year because it was never actually tested against your own circumstances. Comparison is a reasonable source of general inspiration. It's a poor substitute for the specific arithmetic this book asks you to run against your own numbers, in every chapter, every time.

A closing checklist for this chapter

Before considering the tactical foundation of this book complete, it's worth running down the ten mistakes catalogued across this chapter one final time as a simple pass-fail list against your own system: is every percentage tested against a real bad month rather than an average one? Is investment cash actually invested rather than sitting uninvested indefinitely? Is the buffer account genuinely harder to access than ordinary checking? Is the system reviewed on a fixed quarterly schedule rather than left indefinitely alone? Is every account contribution correctly routed to the account it's actually meant for? Does the funding order respect employer match, then high-interest debt, before aggressive discretionary investing? A system that can honestly answer yes to all ten is a system built to last for years, not months — which was, from the very first chapter, the entire point of building it this way in the first place.

Before concluding the tactical foundation of this book as complete, it's worth running down the ten mistakes catalogued across this chapter one final time as a simple pass list [illegible] against your own system: is every percentage tested against a fixed monthly [illegible]? [illegible] actually invested [illegible] rather than sitting [illegible] the buffer [illegible] genuinely [illegible] [illegible] the system [illegible] on a fixed quarterly schedule rather than left to memory alone? [illegible] contribution correctly reported to the account it actually matched? Does the funding order respect employer match, then high-interest debt, before aggressive discretionary investing? [illegible] honestly answered [illegible] all ten [illegible] [illegible] point of building [illegible] in the first place.

Chapter 10 — What to Do When Automation Fails

Why Every Automatic System Needs a Manual Override Protocol

Everything in this book is built to remove the need for manual decisions during normal life. A job loss, a major medical event, a significant emergency isn't normal life — and pretending the automated system should just keep running unchanged through one of these events is its own kind of mistake. This chapter is the deliberate exception to everything that came before it: a manual protocol for the moments the automatic system needs to be actively overridden, not just adjusted.

What's actually happening

An automated system optimized for steady-state life will, left untouched, keep executing exactly the same transfers during a genuine crisis that it executes during a normal month — continuing to move money into investment and buffer-building accounts while checking runs dangerously low, simply because nobody told it to stop. This isn't a flaw in the automation; it's a reminder that automation handles the routine case extremely well and the exceptional case not at all, by design. The exceptional case needs a human decision, made deliberately, not a system that quietly grinds forward regardless of context.

The mistake to avoid isn't having built an automated system in the first place — it's not having a pre-planned protocol for pausing and reprioritizing it when a real disruption hits. Deciding what to do in the middle of a job loss, with no plan already in place, is exactly the high-stress, low-willpower scenario Chapter 1 identified as the worst possible time to make a good financial decision manually. The protocol needs to exist before the crisis, the same way every other mechanic in this book was decided in advance rather than improvised in the moment.

It's worth being precise about what this chapter is and isn't claiming. It isn't claiming that a well-built automated system somehow makes you immune to financial hardship — no system, automated or otherwise, can guarantee that. What it claims is narrower and more useful: that facing a genuine disruption with nine chapters of prior structure already in place

— a funded buffer, clean account separation, a clear sense of what's fixed and what's flexible — puts you in a dramatically better position to respond well than facing the same disruption with no structure at all, scrambling to figure out both what happened financially and what to do about it at the same time. This chapter assumes the first nine chapters' structure is already standing. It's the plan for what happens when that structure meets a force large enough to require deliberate, temporary human intervention rather than continued automatic operation.

The framework: the override sequence

1. Pause new investment contributions first, buffer transfers last. When income drops sharply or stops, the order of what gets paused matters. Long-term investment contributions are the easiest to pause without immediate consequence — money not invested this month can be invested later with essentially no structural harm. Buffer/emergency contributions are the last thing to pause, because the buffer is precisely what's meant to be drawn on during this exact situation; if it's not yet fully funded when the crisis hits, continuing to build it, even at a reduced rate, may still be appropriate depending on severity.

Between those two extremes, discretionary automatic transfers (the flex fund from Chapter 8, for instance) generally pause early and easily.

2. Reverse the account architecture's normal direction. Chapter 3 built accounts so money flows outward from checking into buffer, investing, and goal accounts. During a genuine income disruption, that flow needs to run in reverse: buffer funds move back into checking to cover fixed costs, following the same "one deliberate transfer, not casual access" principle that made the buffer effective in normal times. This isn't a failure of the system — pulling from a fully funded buffer during a real emergency is the buffer doing exactly its job.

3. Recalculate fixed costs against reduced or zero income, immediately, not after the buffer runs low. Waiting to see how bad things get before adjusting spending means the buffer depletes faster than necessary. As soon as an income disruption is confirmed — not "might happen," but confirmed — recalculate which of your fixed costs can actually be reduced or paused (subscriptions from Chapter 5's audit are often the fastest, easiest cuts; larger fixed costs like housing take longer and may not be immediately changeable) and act on the reductions immediately rather than waiting.

4. Set a re-automation trigger for when income resumes. Just as important as the pause sequence is deciding, in advance, what has to be true before the automated system resumes its normal operation — for instance, a full month of stable income at or above the previous baseline, plus the buffer restored to at least half of its prior level, before pay-yourself-first transfers resume at their pre-crisis rate. Without this pre-decided trigger, there's a real risk of either restarting too early (before the situation has actually stabilized) or, more commonly, never consciously restarting at all — the same "temporarily paused becomes permanent" failure mode from Chapter 8, but at a larger scale.

5. Treat the recovery period itself as a re-test of your percentages. Once income has resumed and the buffer is being rebuilt, this is a natural moment to revisit whether the pre-crisis percentages and amounts were actually sustainable, or whether the crisis exposed that they were set too aggressively for a real bad-case scenario. If the buffer wasn't large enough to cover the disruption comfortably, or if fixed costs turned out to have less genuine flexibility than assumed, adjust the system's targets accordingly before simply restoring it to its exact prior state.

Worked example

Someone loses their job with two months of expenses sitting in their buffer account — short of the six-month target, but not nothing. Following the pre-planned sequence: investment contributions pause immediately, the flex fund transfer pauses immediately, and a same-week review of fixed costs identifies $180 a month in subscriptions and services that can be paused or canceled without real hardship. The buffer account begins transferring back into checking on a controlled schedule — not all at once, but at a rate calculated to stretch the two months of reserve closer to three, based on the reduced fixed-cost total.

Job search takes ten weeks. The buffer, stretched by the cost reductions, covers the full gap without needing to be supplemented by debt. Once new income resumes and stabilizes for a full month at a comparable level, the pre-decided re-automation trigger fires: pay-yourself-first transfers resume, but the person also uses this moment, per the framework's fifth point, to rebuild the buffer target from three months of expenses to five, having just experienced firsthand how close two months came to being genuinely insufficient. The system wasn't abandoned by the disruption — it was deliberately paused, used exactly as designed, and consciously restored with a better-calibrated target than it had before.

Partial disruptions: reduced hours, not a full stop

Not every income disruption is a full stop. Reduced hours, a temporary pay cut, or a slow season for variable income (distinct from the extreme swings Chapter 6 already handles) sit in a middle zone between "system runs normally" and "full override protocol." For these partial disruptions, a proportional response tends to work better than either extreme: rather than pausing every automated transfer entirely, scale the pay-yourself-first percentage down by roughly the same proportion income has dropped, keeping the buffer contribution running at a reduced rate rather than stopping it outright, and pausing only the more discretionary automations — the flex fund, any accelerated investment contributions beyond an employer match — first. The same pre-decided trigger for restoring normal operation applies here too: a set number of consecutive normal-income months before scaling back up, decided in advance rather than negotiated with yourself in the moment.

Medical emergencies and the specific complications they add

A medical emergency often combines an income disruption with a large, immediate expense at the same time, which can outpace even a well-funded buffer faster than a job loss alone would. Where this book's general override sequence still applies — pause discretionary and investment automation first, preserve buffer access — a medical situation specifically also benefits from checking, immediately rather than after the fact, whether payment plans, financial assistance programs, or billing negotiation are available through the provider or facility before assuming the full cost has to come from the buffer or from debt. Healthcare billing in many systems has more room for negotiation and structured payment than people initially assume, and asking early — before a bill goes to collections or accrues additional cost — tends to produce meaningfully better outcomes than waiting. This isn't a mechanic this book can fully automate, since it depends heavily on individual circumstances and the specific provider or system involved, but it belongs explicitly in the override protocol as a step to check, not skip, in the moment a medical emergency actually happens.

A second worked example: a partial-hours disruption

A worker's hours are cut by a quarter for what the employer describes as a temporary, three-to-four-month slowdown. Rather than treating this as full-scale crisis, they scale their pay-yourself-first rate down proportionally — from 12% to 9% — and pause only the flex fund transfer, leaving the buffer contribution and the employer-matched retirement contribution running at their normal rate, since neither of those is genuinely at risk during a reduction of this size once the discretionary layer has already been trimmed. They set a calendar trigger for four months out to review whether hours have been restored; when they are, the system reverts to its normal rate without needing a broader reassessment, because the disruption was proportional and the response was sized to match it rather than treated as a full override event.

Writing the protocol down before you need it

Everything in this chapter assumes the override sequence has already been decided in advance, and it's worth being explicit about what "decided" should actually mean in practice: written down somewhere accessible, not just generally understood in your own head. A short document — even a single page — listing the pause order (discretionary automations first, buffer transfers last), the fixed-cost reduction targets you'd act on, and the specific conditions that trigger re-automation, means that during an actual crisis, when stress is highest and decision-making capacity is lowest — exactly the condition Chapter 1 identified as the worst time to make a financial decision from scratch — there's a document to follow rather than a plan to reconstruct from memory under pressure.

This also matters for anyone else who shares financial responsibility with you. If a partner, family member, or anyone else would need to help execute this protocol during a crisis you're not able to manage yourself — a serious illness, an emergency that affects your own capacity to act — a written protocol they can follow without needing you to explain the logic in the moment is significantly more useful than a system that only exists in your head. Treat this document the same way you'd treat any other emergency preparation: written once, during a calm period, reviewed occasionally, and available when the exact situation it was built for actually arrives.

Distinguishing a disruption from a permanent change

Not every income shock is temporary, and treating a permanent change as though it were a temporary disruption is its own distinct mistake, separate from everything covered so far in this chapter. A layoff that leads to a genuinely lower-paying role, a career change, an injury that permanently affects earning capacity — these aren't situations where the override protocol's pause-and-resume logic applies cleanly, because there's no prior baseline to resume once the dust settles. The signal to watch for: if, several months into what was assumed to be a temporary disruption, the new income level shows no sign of returning toward the old baseline, that's the cue to stop treating the situation as a pause and start treating it as a full system rebuild

— revisiting fixed costs, account structures, and every percentage in this book from scratch against the new reality, rather than continuing to wait for a resumption that isn't coming. This isn't a failure of the system or the protocol; it's simply a different situation that calls for a different response, and recognizing which situation you're actually in, honestly and reasonably promptly, prevents months of a paused system quietly draining a buffer that was never going to be replenished under the old assumptions.

The role of insurance and benefits in reducing how often the override protocol gets used

Everything in this chapter is about what to do once a disruption has already happened. It's worth noting, briefly, that some of these disruptions are themselves insurable or partially mitigated by benefits many people already have access to but don't fully account for when building their buffer targets — short- and long-term disability coverage, unemployment benefits where available, health insurance that caps out-of-pocket exposure. None of this eliminates the need for a buffer or an override protocol, but a realistic accounting of what coverage you already have can meaningfully affect how large a buffer genuinely needs to be, and how severe a given disruption is actually likely to get before other support kicks in. This is worth a specific line item in your periodic system review: confirming what coverage exists, what it would actually pay out and when, and whether the buffer target from Chapter 3 has been sized with that coverage already accounted for, or is unknowingly padding for a risk that's already partially covered elsewhere.

Rehearsing the protocol before it's needed

A fire drill is valuable specifically because it's practiced before an actual fire, when there's no smoke, no urgency, and no risk in getting a step wrong. The override protocol in this chapter benefits from the same kind of low-stakes rehearsal. Once a year, as part of an annual (not quarterly) portion of your system review, walk through the protocol as a thought exercise: if income stopped entirely next month, what would actually happen, step by step, following the pause sequence, the account-flow reversal, and the fixed-cost review outlined earlier in this chapter? Which specific automations would you pause first? How many months would the current buffer actually stretch, given current fixed costs, not the fixed costs from whenever the buffer target was last calculated? This isn't meant to induce anxiety — it's meant to catch gaps in the plan while there's no pressure attached to finding them. A protocol that's only ever been theoretical, never walked through even hypothetically, tends to reveal its gaps for the first time during the actual crisis it was meant to handle smoothly. A protocol rehearsed annually, on paper, during a calm month, reveals those same gaps far earlier and far more cheaply.

The full system, viewed as a whole

Ten chapters in, it's worth stepping back and seeing the complete shape of what's been built, because each chapter in isolation can start to feel like a separate tool rather than a piece of one integrated design. The account architecture from Chapter 3 is the skeleton. The pay-yourself-first mechanics from Chapter 2 and the investment automation from Chapter 4 are what actually moves through that skeleton on a predictable schedule. The subscription audit from Chapter 5 patches the leaks that would otherwise drain the system from the spending side. The variable-income structure from Chapter 6 is the adapter that lets the whole system run even when the input itself isn't steady. Escalation from Chapter 7 is the mechanism that keeps the system's output scaling with your life instead of falling behind it. Flexibility from Chapter 8 is what keeps the system from snapping the first time real life doesn't cooperate. The tactical mistakes catalog in Chapter 9 is the maintenance manual. And this chapter, the override protocol, is what happens when the system meets a shock large enough that none of the other chapters' built-in flexibility is sufficient on its own. None of these pieces does much good in isolation. Together, they're a complete, self-sustaining structure — which was the entire goal from the first page of this book.

What comes after the override

Once the override protocol has run its course and normal operation resumes, it's worth treating the disruption itself as useful data rather than simply an episode to move past and forget. Every real disruption reveals something a purely hypothetical planning exercise couldn't: whether the buffer target was actually large enough, whether the pause sequence was ordered sensibly for what you actually needed most, whether fixed costs had more flexibility than assumed or less. Fold these lessons back into the system deliberately, during the recovery-period retest this chapter already recommends, rather than letting the experience fade into a vague memory of "that hard stretch" without changing anything concrete about how the system is built. A system that's weathered one real disruption and been recalibrated in response to it is measurably more robust than a system that's only ever been tested on paper — treat the first real crisis, uncomfortable as it is while it's happening, as the system's most valuable stress test, and make sure it actually teaches the system something before moving on.

Closing

Nothing in this book asked you to want to save money more, spend less, or feel differently about the temptation to buy things you don't need. That's deliberate. Wanting the right thing has never been the part that was actually missing — most people already want to build savings, invest consistently, and stop bleeding money to forgotten subscriptions. What's been missing is a structure that doesn't require that wanting to survive every single decision point, every single month, indefinitely, without a single bad week.

The system in this book works by removing as many of those decision points as possible and replacing them with structure: money that moves before you can spend it, accounts that separate by job instead of blurring into one number, contributions that happen on a schedule instead of waiting for a feeling of readiness, savings rates that rise with your income instead of getting quietly outpaced by it, and a pre-planned protocol for the moments a real crisis means the automatic system needs a deliberate human override.

None of this requires more discipline than you already have. It requires less of it — because the whole point is that discipline is no longer the thing holding the system up. The accounts, the transfers, and the triggers are.

If you're deciding where to actually start, rather than trying to implement all ten chapters simultaneously, a reasonable order looks like this: build the account architecture from Chapter 3 first, since almost nothing else in this book works without it. Set a pay-yourself-first percentage from Chapter 2, tested honestly against a bad month rather than an aspirational one. Automate your investment contribution per Chapter 4, at minimum capturing any employer match available to you. Run one full recurring-cost audit from Chapter 5 to see what it recovers. If your income is variable, build the two-layer structure from Chapter 6 before anything else, since the rest of the book assumes a stable paycheck that variable income doesn't actually have until that structure exists. From there, layer in escalation, flexibility, and the failure protocol as your situation calls for them — none of them require the others to already be perfect, and a partially built system that's actually running beats a perfectly designed one that's still sitting in a planning document.

It's worth being honest about what this book can't do. It can't guarantee a specific outcome, because outcomes depend on income, timeline, market conditions, and dozens of factors outside any system's control. What it can do — and what it was built specifically to do — is guarantee that the behavior underneath the outcome happens consistently, every month, regardless of how you're feeling about money that particular week. That consistency is the entire lever available to you, and it's a real one. Two people with identical incomes, one running this system and one running on willpower alone, will not end up in the same place after ten years, even if both of them wanted the same outcome equally badly on day one. The difference won't be that one of them wanted it more. It'll be that one of them built a structure that didn't need the wanting to survive, and the other one's plan quietly needed it every single month, for ten years straight, without a single exception.

You don't need ten years of exceptional willpower. You need one afternoon to build the structure, and then a quarterly hour to keep it honest. That's the trade this book is offering, and it's a good one.

One more thing worth carrying with you past the last page: this system is meant to fade into the background of your life, not become a new preoccupation. The goal was never to turn you into someone who thinks about money constantly, checking balances daily or obsessing over percentages. It was the opposite — to build a structure sturdy enough that you can go back to thinking about your actual life, your work, your relationships, the things that matter more than any of this, while the accounts and transfers keep doing their job underneath, unattended, exactly as designed. If this book has done its work, the measure of success isn't that you think about money more carefully. It's that you think about it less, because there's less left to think about.

Build it once. Test each piece against your worst realistic month, not your best one. Review it quarterly, not daily. And when life genuinely disrupts it, follow the override protocol you decided on ahead of time, rather than improvising in the moment you're least equipped to improvise well.

That's the whole system. It doesn't need you to be a different person than you already are. It just needs to run.

Notes & Further Reading

This book intentionally avoids citing specific interest rates, contribution limits, account minimums, or app names, since these change frequently and any specific figure would be stale within a year or two of publication. Verify current numbers, limits, and account features directly with your bank, brokerage, or employer plan administrator before acting.

Readers interested in the broader ideas this book builds on may find the following genuinely useful:

- **"Nudge" by Richard H. Thaler and Cass R. Sunstein** — the foundational text on choice architecture and default effects, including the mechanics behind automatic-enrollment retirement savings programs, which is the closest academic cousin to this book's core argument that defaults do more work than willpower. - **"Your Money or Your Life" by Vicki Robin (with Joe Dominguez)** — an early and influential articulation of treating money as a values-and-systems question rather than a pure budgeting exercise. - **"I Will Teach You to Be Rich" by Ramit Sethi** — a widely read practical guide to automated personal finance systems, conscious spending plans, and account structuring, closely adjacent to the mechanics covered in this book. - **"The Psychology of Money" by Morgan Housel** — useful context on why financial behavior is driven more by psychology than by spreadsheets, complementary to (though distinct in focus from) the tactical, mechanics-first approach of this book. - **Consumer Financial Protection Bureau (consumerfinance.gov)** — a genuinely useful, non-commercial public resource for understanding account types, consumer protections, and general financial planning concepts referenced throughout this book, with information kept current by a federal agency rather than a single author's memory. - **"The Behavior Gap" by Carl Richards** — a short, plainly written book on the recurring gap between what people know they should do with money and what they actually do, useful context for why a mechanics-first, decision-removing approach tends to outperform advice aimed purely at better decision-making in the moment. - **"Atomic Habits" by James Clear** — while not a finance book specifically, its treatment of environment design and habit-formation mechanics (making good behavior obvious and easy, making poor behavior invisible and hard) parallels the friction-based logic this book applies specifically to money.

Two categories of resource are deliberately left out of this list. First, specific banks, apps, or brokerage platforms — any recommendation here would be a snapshot of a competitive market that reshuffles constantly, and a stale product recommendation ages worse than no recommendation at all. When evaluating a specific institution for any of the four account roles in Chapter 3, judge it against this book's structural criteria (transfer friction, fee structure, yield competitiveness) rather than a brand name, and re-verify those criteria periodically, since a good fit today isn't guaranteed to stay a good fit indefinitely. Second, specific interest rates, contribution limits, or tax figures — these are set and periodically adjusted by financial institutions and tax authorities respectively, and the only reliable source for a current figure is the institution or agency itself at the time you're actually setting up an account, not a book written at an earlier point in time.

For readers whose primary obstacle isn't building the system described here, but understanding *why* they've avoided or delayed doing so — chronic postponement of financial decisions despite already knowing what to do — the companion territory of that psychological pattern is covered elsewhere, outside the scope of this book, which is deliberately limited to mechanics rather than diagnosis.

A final note on verification. Every mechanic in this book — pay-yourself-first sequencing, account separation, dollar-cost averaging as a byproduct of scheduled contributions, buffer sizing, escalation timing — describes a structural principle that you can verify directly against your own bank statements, your own account behavior, and your own tested numbers, rather than a claim that asks you to simply trust the author. Where this book makes a claim about how money behaves psychologically — that a visible balance reads as spendable regardless of its intended purpose, for instance — that claim is testable against your own experience and is deliberately kept general enough not to depend on a specific study or statistic that could go stale or be misremembered. This is by design: a book about removing dependence on things that can fail you (willpower, memory, motivation) should not itself depend on things that can fail the reader (an uncheckable statistic, a citation that doesn't hold up, a fabricated source). Everything here is meant to be checked, not simply believed.

About the Author

Daniel Cross writes about the mechanics of money — the concrete systems, structures, and scripts that make good financial decisions automatic rather than aspirational. He is the author of the Wealth Mechanics series, covering negotiation, debt payoff, pricing, and automated savings systems, each focused on a distinct, executable set of tactics rather than a general theory of personal finance. His approach is shaped by years spent building financial systems for people who already knew what they should be doing and needed a structure that didn't depend on remembering to do it.

Each book in the Wealth Mechanics series stands on its own and covers a single, closed domain — a specific set of tactics you can put to use immediately, without needing to have read the others first. Readers who want the full toolkit, from negotiating what you're worth to building the automated system that grows it without ongoing effort, will find the rest of the series covers the adjacent ground this book deliberately leaves alone: negotiation and pricing conversations, structured debt payoff, and the pricing mechanics of freelance and creative work. Where Money Instinct diagnoses the psychological patterns that make money decisions hard, Wealth Mechanics hands you the concrete, repeatable systems for acting once the decision is made — this book's contribution to that toolkit is the one piece of infrastructure that, once built, makes every other good financial decision require nothing further from you at all.

Also in the Series

Every book in Wealth Mechanics stands on its own — read them in any order. If this one was useful, the library continues:

The Negotiation Playbook

The Debt Freedom System

The Pricing Playbook

The Savings Rate Playbook

The Investment Onboarding Playbook

The Side Income Playbook

The Real Estate Entry Playbook

The Tax Reduction Playbook

The Equity Compensation Playbook

www.ingramcontent.com/pod-product-compliance
Lightning Source LLC
LaVergne TN
LVHW010719061126
851857LV00014B/1256
9781804281239